2 PETER

THE
TEACHER'S
OUTLINE & STUDY
BIBLE

2 PETER

THE

TEACHER'S

OUTLINE & STUDY

BIBLE

NEW TESTAMENT

KING JAMES VERSION

Leadership Ministries Worldwide
PO Box 21310
Chattanooga, TN 37424-0310

Please address all requests for information or permission to:
    Leadership Ministries Worldwide
    PO Box 21310
    Chattanooga TN 37424-0310
    Ph.# (423) 855-2181   FAX (423) 855-8616   E•Mail 74152,616@compuserve.org.
    http://www.goshen.net/OutlineBible

Library of Congress Catalog Card Number: 94-073070
International Standard Book Number: 1-57407-019-3

PRINTED IN THE U.S.A.

PUBLISHED BY LEADERSHIP MINISTRIES WORLDWIDE

H O W T O U S E

THE TEACHER'S OUTLINE AND STUDY BIBLE (TOSB)

To gain maximum benefit, here is all you do. Follow these easy steps, using the sample outline below.

1 STUDY TITLE

2 MAJOR POINTS

3 SUB-POINTS

**4 COMMENTARY, QUES-
TIONS, APPLICATION,
ILLUSTRATIONS**
(Follows Scripture)

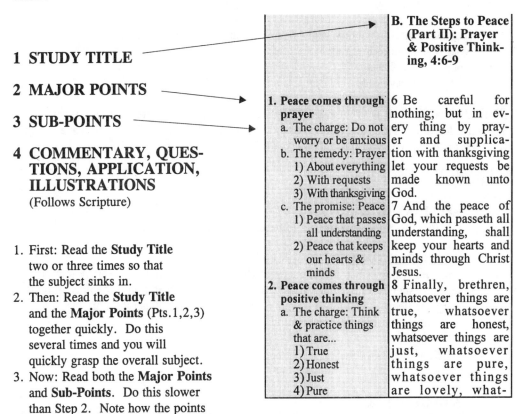

B. The Steps to Peace (Part II): Prayer & Positive Thinking, 4:6-9

1. Peace comes through prayer
a. The charge: Do not worry or be anxious
b. The remedy: Prayer
  1) About everything
  2) With requests
  3) With thanksgiving
c. The promise: Peace
  1) Peace that passes all understanding
  2) Peace that keeps our hearts & minds
2. Peace comes through positive thinking
a. The charge: Think & practice things that are...
  1) True
  2) Honest
  3) Just
  4) Pure

6 Be careful for nothing; but in every thing by prayer and supplication with thanksgiving let your requests be made known unto God.
7 And the peace of God, which passeth all understanding, shall keep your hearts and minds through Christ Jesus.
8 Finally, brethren, whatsoever things are true, whatsoever things are honest, whatsoever things are just, whatsoever things are pure, whatsoever things are lovely, what-

1. First: Read the **Study Title** two or three times so that the subject sinks in.
2. Then: Read the **Study Title** and the **Major Points** (Pts.1,2,3) together quickly. Do this several times and you will quickly grasp the overall subject.
3. Now: Read both the **Major Points** and **Sub-Points**. Do this slower than Step 2. Note how the points are beside the applicable verse, and simply state what the Scripture is saying—in Outline form.
4. Read the **Commentary**. As you read and re-read, pray that the Holy Spirit will bring to your attention exactly what you should study and teach. It's all there, outlined and fully developed, just waiting for you to study and teach.

<u>TEACHERS, PLEASE NOTE</u>:

⇒ Cover the **Scripture** and the **Major Points** with your students. Drive the **Scripture** and **Major Points** into their hearts and minds.

(Please continue on next page)

⇒ Cover *only some of the commentary* with your students, not all (unless of course you have plenty of time). Cover only as much commentary as is needed to get the major points across.

⇒ Do NOT feel that you must...
- cover all the commentary under each point
- share every illustration
- ask all the questions

An abundance of commentary is given so you can find just what you need for...
- your own style of teaching
- your own emphasis
- your own class needs

PLEASE NOTE: It is of utmost importance that you (and your study group) grasp the Scripture, the Study Title, and Major Points. It is this that the Holy Spirit will make alive to your heart and that you will more likely remember and use day by day.

MAJOR POINTS include:

APPLICATIONS:
Use these to show how the Scripture applies to everyday life.

ILLUSTRATIONS:
Simply a window that allows enough light in the lesson so a point can be more clearly seen. A suggestion: Do not just "read" through an illustration if the illustration is a story, but learn it and make it your own. Then give the illustration life by communicating it with *excitement & energy*.

QUESTIONS:
These are designed to stimulate thought and discussion.

A CLOSER LOOK:
In some of the studies, you will see a portion boxed in and entitled: "A Closer Look." This discussion will be a closer study on a particular point. It is generally too detailed for a Sunday School class session, but more adaptable for personal study or an indepth Bible Study class.

PERSONAL JOURNAL:
At the close of every lesson there is space for you to record brief thoughts regarding the impact of the lesson on your life. As you study through the Bible, you will find these comments invaluable as you look back upon them.

Now, may our wonderful Lord bless you mightily as you study and teach His Holy Word. And may our Lord grant you much fruit: many who will become greater servants and witnesses for Him.

REMEMBER!

The Teacher's Outline & Study Bible is the only study material that actually outlines the Bible verse by verse for you right beside the Scripture. As you accumulate the various books of The Teacher's Outline & Study Bible for your study and teaching, you will have the Bible outlined book by book, passage by passage, and verse by verse.

The outlines alone makes saving every book a must! (Also encourage your students, if you are teaching, to keep their student edition. They also have the unique verse by verse outline of Scripture in their version.)

Just think for a moment. Over the course of your life, you will have your very own personalized commentary of the Bible. No other book besides the Bible will mean as much to you because it will contain your insights, your struggles, your victories, and your recorded moments with the Lord.

"Study to show thyself approved unto God, a workman that needeth not to be ashamed, rightly dividing the word of truth" (2 Tim.2:15).

"All scripture is given by inspiration of God, and is profitable for doctrine, for reproof, for correction, for instruction in righteousness: that the man of God may be perfect, throughly furnished unto all good works" (2 Tim.3:16-17).

*** All direct quotes are followed by a Superscript Footnote number. The credit information for each Footnote is listed at the bottom of the page.

MISCELLANEOUS ABBREVIATIONS

&	=	And
Bckgrd.	=	Background
Bc.	=	Because
Circ.	=	Circumstance
Concl.	=	Conclusion
Cp.	=	Compare
Ct.	=	Contrast
Dif.	=	Different
e.g.	=	For example
Et.	=	Eternal
Govt.	=	Government
Id.	=	Identity or Identification
Illust.	=	Illustration
K.	=	Kingdom, K. of God, K. of Heaven, etc.
No.	=	Number
N.T.	=	New Testament
O.T.	=	Old Testament
Pt.	=	Point
Quest.	=	Question
Rel.	=	Religion
Resp.	=	Responsibility
Rev.	=	Revelation
Rgt.	=	Righteousness
Thru	=	Through
V.	=	Verse
Vs.	=	Verses

Publisher & Distributor

DEDICATED:

To all the men and women of the world
who preach and teach the Gospel of our
Lord Jesus Christ
and
To the Mercy and Grace of God.

——————— *&* ———————

- Demonstrated to us in Christ Jesus our Lord.

  "In whom we have redemption through His
  blood, the forgiveness of sins, according to the
  riches of His grace." (Eph. 1:7)

- Out of the mercy and grace of God His Word has
  flowed. Let every person know that God will have
  mercy upon him, forgiving and using him to fulfill
  His glorious plan of salvation.

  "For God so loved the world, that he gave his only
  begotten Son, that whosoever believeth in him should
  not perish, but have everlasting life. For God sent not
  his Son into the world to condemn the world; but that
  the world through him might be saved." (Jn 3:16-17)

  "For this is good and acceptable in the sight of God
  our Saviour; who will have all men to be saved, and to
  come unto the knowledge of the truth." (I Tim. 2:3-4)

——————— *&* ———————

The Teacher's Outline and Study Bible™
is written for God's people to use
in their study and teaching of God's Holy Word.

LEADERSHIP MINISTRIES WORLDWIDE

OUR FIVEFOLD MISSION & PURPOSE:

- To share the Word of God with the world.
- To help the believer, both minister and layman alike, in his understanding, preaching, and teaching of God's Word.
- To do everything we possibly can to lead men, women, boys, and girls to give their hearts and lives to Jesus Christ and to secure the eternal life which He offers.
- To do all we can to minister to the needy of the world.
- To give Jesus Christ His proper place, the place which the Word gives Him. Therefore — No work of Leadership Ministries Worldwide will ever be personalized.

This material, like similar works, has come from imperfect man and is thus susceptible to human error. We are nevertheless grateful to God for both calling us and empowering us through His Holy Spirit to undertake this task. Because of His goodness and grace, **The Preacher's Outline & Sermon Bible®** - New Testament is complete in 14 volumes as well as the single volume of **The Minister's Handbook**.

God has given the strength and stamina to bring us this far. Our confidence is that, as we keep our eyes on Him and grounded in the undeniable truths of the Word, we will continue working through the Old Testament Volumes and produce periodically a new series known as **The Teacher's Outline & Study Bible™**. CD-ROM and Internet distribution is mak- ing all these great materials available electronically, anywhere in the world.

To everyone, everywhere who preaches and teaches the Word, we offer this material firstly to Him in whose name we labor and serve, and for whose glory it has been produced.

Our daily prayer is that each volume will lead thousands, millions, yes even billions, into a better understanding of the Holy Scriptures and a fuller knowledge of Jesus Christ the incarnate Word, of whom the Scriptures so faithfully testify.

• *Equipping God's Servants Worldwide with OUTLINE Bible Materials* •

LMW is a 501(c)(3) nonprofit, international nondenominational mission agency   9/98

LEADERSHIP
MINISTRIES
WORLDWIDE

P.O. Box 21310, 515 Airport Road, Suite 107
Chattanooga, TN 37424-0310
(423) 855-2181 FAX (423) 855-87616
E-Mail - outlinebible@compuserve.com
www.outlinebible.org [Free download samples]

ACKNOWLEDGMENTS

Every child of God is precious to the Lord and deeply loved. And every child as a
servant of the Lord touches the lives of those who come in contact with him or his ministry.
The writing ministry of the following servants have touched this work, and we are grateful that
God brought their writings our way. We hereby acknowledge their ministry to us, being fully
aware that there are so many others down through the years whose writings have touched our
lives and who deserve mention, but the weaknesses of our minds have caused them to fade from
memory. May our wonderful Lord continue to bless the ministry of these dear servants, and the
ministry of us all as we diligently labor to reach the world for Christ and to meet the desperate
needs of those who suffer so much.

THE GREEK SOURCES

1   Expositor's Greek Testament, Edited by W. Robertson Nicoll. Grand
        Rapids, MI: Eerdmans
        Publishing Co., 1970

2.   Robertson, A.T. Word Pictures in the New Testament. Nashville,
        TN: Broadman Press, 1930.

3.   Thayer, Joseph Henry. Greek-English Lexicon of the New Testament.
        New York: American Book Co.

4.   Vincent, Marvin R. Word Studies in the New Testament. Grand
        Rapids, MI: Eerdmans Publishing Co., 1969.

5.   Vine, W.E. Expository Dictionary of New Testament Words. Old
        Tappan, NJ: Fleming H. Revell Co.

6.   Wuest, Kenneth S. Word Studies in the Greek New Testament. Grand
        Rapids, MI: Eerdmans Publishing Co., 1953.

THE REFERENCE WORKS

7.   Cruden's Complete Concordance of the Old & New Testament.
        Philadelphia, PA: The John C. Winston Co., 1930.

8.   Josephus' Complete Works. Grand Rapids, MI: Kregel Publications,
        1981.

9.   Lockyer, Herbert, Series of Books, including his Books on All the
        Men, Women, Miracles, and Parables of the Bible. Grand Rapids,
        MI: Zondervan Publishing House.

10.   Nave's Topical Bible. Nashville, TN: The Southewstern Co.

11.   The Amplified New Testament. (Scripture Quotations are from the
        Amplified New Testament, Copyright 1954, 1958, 1987 by the
        Lockman Foundation. Used by permission.)

12. The Four Translation New Testament (Including King James, New American Standard, Williams - New Testament In the Language of the People, Beck - New Testament In the Language of Today.) Minneapolis, MN: World Wide Publications.

13. The New Compact Bible Dictionary, Edited by T. Alton Bryant. Grand Rapids, MI: Zondervan Publishing House, 1967.

14. The New Thompson Chain Reference Bible. Indianapolis, IN: B.B. Kirkbride Bible Co., 1964,

THE COMMENTARIES

15. Barclay, William. Daily Study Bible Series. Philadelphia, PA: Westminster Press.

16. Bruce, F.F. The Epistle to the Colossians. Westwood, NJ: Fleming H. Revell Co., 1968.

17. Bruce, F.F. Epistle to the Hebrews.Grand Rapids, MI: Eerdmans Publishing Co., 1964.

18. Bruce, F.F. The Epistles of John. Old Tappan, NJ: Fleming H. Revell Co., 1970.

19. Criswell, W.A. Expository Sermons on Revelation. Grand Rapids, MI: Zondervan Publishing House, 1962-66.

20. Greene, Oliver. The Epistles of John. Greenville, SC: The Gospel Hour, Inc., 1966.

21. Greene, Oliver. The Epistles of Paul the Apostle to the Hebrews. Greenville, SC: The Gospel Hour, Inc., 1965.

22. Greene, Oliver. The Epistles of Paul the Apostle to Timothy & Titus. Greenville, SC: The Gospel Hour, Inc., 1964.

23. Greene, Oliver. The Revelation Verse by Verse Study. Greenville, SC: The Gospel Hour, Inc., 1963.

24. Henry, Matthew. Commentary on the Whole Bible. Old Tappan, NJ: Fleming H. Revell Co.

25. Hodge, Charles. Exposition on Romans & on Corinthians. Grand Rapids, MI: Eerdmans Publishing Co., 1972-1973.

26. Ladd, George Eldon. A Commentary On the Revelation of John. Grand Rapids, MI: Eerdmans Publishing Co., 1972-1973.

27. Leupold, H.C. Exposition of Daniel. Grand Rapids, MI: Baker Book House, 1969.

28. Newell, William R. Hebrews, Verse by Verse. Chicago, IL: Moody Press.

29. Strauss, Lehman. Devotional Studies in Philippians. Neptune, NJ: Loizeaux Brothers.

30. Strauss, Lehman. Colossians & 1 timothy. Neptune, NJ: Loizeaux Brothers.

31. Strauss, Lehman. The Book of the Revelation. Neptune, NJ: Loizeaux Brothers.

32. The New Testament & Wycliffe Bible Commentary, Edited by Charles F. Pfeiffer & Everett F. Harrison. New York: The Iverson Associates, 1971. Produced for Moody Monthly. Chicago Moody Press, 1962.

33. The Pulpit Commentary, Edited by H.D.M. Spence & Joseph S. Exell. Grand Rapids, MI: Eerdmans's Publishing Co., 1950.

34. Thomas, W.H. Griffith. Hebrews, A Devotional Commentary. Grand Rapids, MI: Eerdman's Publishing Co., 1970.

35. Thomas, W.H. Griffith. Studies in Colossians & Philemon. Grand Rapids, MI: Baker Book House, 1973.

36. Tyndale New Testament Commentaries. Grand Rapids, MI: Eerdman's Publishing Co., Began in 1958.

37. Walker, Thomas. Acts of the Apostles. Chicago, IL: Moody Press, 1965.

38. Walvoord, John. The Thessalonian Epistles. Grand Rapids, MI: Zondervan Publishing House, 1973.

OTHER SOURCES

39. Green, Michael P. Illustrations for Biblical Preaching. Grand Rapids, MI: Baker Books, 1996.

40. Knight, Walter B. Knight's Master Book of 4,000 Illustrations. Grand Rapids, MI: Eerdmans Publishing Company, 1994.

41. Lucado, Max. And the Angels Were Silent. Portland, OR: Multnomah Press, 1992.

42. Tan, Paul Lee. Encyclopedia of 7,700 Illustrations: Signs of the Times. Rockville, MD: Assurance Publishers, 1985.

43. Warren W. Wiersbe. The Bible Exposition Commentary, Vol.2. Wheaton, IL: Victor Books, 1989.

Currently Available Materials, with New Volumes Releasing Regularly

- **THE PREACHER'S OUTLINE & SERMON BIBLE® — DELUXE EDITION**

  Volume 1 . . . . St. Matthew I (chapters 1-15)   3-Ring, looseleaf binder
  Volume 2 . . . . St. Matthew II (chapters 16-28)
  Volume 3 . . . . St. Mark
  Volume 4 . . . . St. Luke
  Volume 5 . . . . St. John
  Volume 6 . . . . Acts
  Volume 7 . . . . Romans
  Volume 8 . . . . 1, 2 Corinthians (1 volume)
  Volume 9 . . . . Galatians, Ephesians, Philippians, Colossians (1 volume)
  Volume 10 . . . . 1,2 Thessalonians, 1,2 Timothy, Titus, Philemon (1 volume)
  Volume 11 . . . . Hebrews -James (1 volume)
  Volume 12 . . . . 1,2 Peter, 1,2,3 John, Jude (1 volume)
  Volume 13 . . . . Revelation
  Volume 14 . . . . Master Outline & Subject Index

  FULL SET — 14 Volumes

- **THE PREACHER'S OUTLINE & SERMON BIBLE® — OLD TESTAMENT**

  Volume 1 . . . . Genesis I (chapters 1-11)
  Volume 2 . . . . Genesis II (chapters 12-50)
  Volume 3 . . . . Exodus I (chapters 1-18)
  Volume 4 . . . . Exodus II (chapters 19-40)
  Volume 5 . . . . Leviticus   New volumes release periodically

- **THE PREACHER'S OUTLINE & SERMON BIBLE® — SOFTBOUND EDITION**
  Identical content as Deluxe above. Lightweight, compact, and affordable for overseas & traveling

- **THE PREACHER'S OUTLINE & SERMON BIBLE® — 3 VOL HARDCOVER w/CD**

- **THE PREACHER'S OUTLINE & SERMON BIBLE® — NIV SOFTBOUND EDITION**

- **The Minister's Personal Handbook - What the Bible Says...to the Minister**
  12 Chapters - 127 Subjects - 400 Verses *OUTLINED* - Paperback, Leatherette, 3-ring

- **THE TEACHER'S OUTLINE & STUDY BIBLE™ • New Testament Books •**
  Complete 45 minute lessons - 4 months of studies/book; 200± pages - Student Journal Guides

- **OUTLINE Bible Studies series: 10 Commandments - The Tabernacle**

- **Practical Word Studies: New Testament - 2,000 Key Words Made Easy**

- **CD-ROM: Preacher, Teacher, and Handbook-** (Windows/STEP) - **WORD***Search*

- **Translations of Preacher, Teacher, and Minister's Handbook: <u>Limited Quantities</u>**
  Russian — Spanish — Korean Future: French, Portuguese, Hindi, Chinese
  — *Contact us for Specific Language Availability and Prices* —

For quantity orders and information, please contact either:

LEADERSHIP MINISTRIES WORLDWIDE   *Your OUTLINE Bible Bookseller*
PO Box 21310
Chattanooga, TN 37424-0310
(423) 855-2181 (9am - 5pm Eastern) • FAX (423) 855-8616 (24 hours)
E•Mail - outlinebible@compuserve.com.

⇢ FREE Download Sample Pages — www.outlinebible.org

• *Equipping God's Servants Worldwide with OUTLINE Bible Materials* •
LMW is a nonprofit, international, nondenominational mission agency   9/98

"
Go ye therefore, and
teach all nations
" (Mt. 28:19)

A SPECIAL NOTE FOR THE BIBLE STUDY LEADER, PASTOR OR MINISTER OF EDUCATION

The teaching material that you have before you gives your church the *maximum flexibility* in scheduling for the church year or for any Bible study program. If you prefer not to follow a self-paced schedule, please note:

To Begin Your Exciting Study, Follow These Simple LESSON PLANS FOR 2 PETER 1 QUARTER OR 13 WEEKS

I. THE GREAT SALVATION OF GOD, 1:1-21

WEEK #	LESSON TITLE	SCRIPTURE TEXT	PAGE NUMBER
1	*"The Great Gift of Christ the Messiah:Salvation"*	1:1-4 (Points 1 & 2)	15
2	*"The Great Gift of Christ the Messiah: Salvation"*	1:1-4 (Points 3-5)	19
3	*"The Great Things of a Believer's Life"*	1:5-15 (Point 1)	26
4	*"The Great Things of a Believer's Life"*	1:5-15 (Points 2-3)	31
5	*"The Great Proof of Salvation"*	1:16-21	37

II. THE WARNING AGAINST FALSE TEACHERS, 2:1-22

WEEK #	LESSON TITLE	SCRIPTURE TEXT	PAGE NUMBER
6	*"The Description & Judgment of False Teachers"*	2:1-9	48
7	*"The Character & Conduct of False Teachers"*	2:10-22 (Points 1-5)	58
8	*"The Character & Conduct of False Teachers"*	2:10-22 (Points 6-10)	63
9	*"The Character & Conduct of False Teachers"*	2:10-22 (Points 11-15)	66

III. THE SECOND COMING OF CHRIST AND THE END OF THE WORLD, 3:1-18

WEEK #	LESSON TITLE	SCRIPTURE TEXT	PAGE NUMBER
10	*"The First Thing to Know: Scoffers Shall Come"*	3:1-7	71
11	*"The One Thing Not to be Ignorant About: Why Christ Has Not Yet Returned"*	3:8-10	80
12	*"The Things Believers Must Do Since Jesus Christ is Coming Again (Part I)*	3:11-14	88
13	*"The Things Believers Must Do Since Jesus Christ is Coming Again (Part II)*	3:15-18	95

OUTLINE OF 2 PETER

THE TEACHER'S OUTLINE & SERMON BIBLE is *unique*. It differs from all other Study Bibles & Sermon Resource Materials in that every Passage and Subject is outlined right beside the Scripture. When you choose any *Subject* below and turn to the reference, you have not only the Scripture, but you discover the Scripture and Subject *already outlined for you--verse by verse*.

For a quick example, choose one of the subjects below and turn over to the Scripture, and you will find this marvelous help for faster, easier, and more accurate use.

A suggestion: For the quickest overview of 2 Peter, first read *all the major titles* (I, II, III, etc.), then come back and read the sub-titles.

OUTLINE OF 2 PETER

THE SECOND EPISTLE GENERAL OF
PETER

INTRODUCTION

<u>**AUTHOR**</u>: Simon Peter, the Apostle (2 Pt.1:1). However, note several facts. (Much of the following is taken from Michael Green. He makes an excellent and scholarly case for Peter's authorship.) (*The Second Epistle of Peter and The Epistle of Jude.* "The Tyndale New Testament Commentaries," ed. by RVG Tasker. Grand Rapids, MI: Eerdmans, 1968, p.13f).

   1.   The author is questioned by many commentators. The questioning centers primarily around external evidence such as the following two facts.

      ⇒   There are no direct references to the book by the earliest Christian writers.

      ⇒   The first person to mention Second Peter by name was Origen who lived around the middle of the third century.

When all of the evidence is considered, however, it points to Peter being the author.

     a. The earliest church fathers do have statements that are similar to parts of II Peter: I Clement (A.D. 950), II Clement (A.D. 150), Aristides (A.D. 130), Valentinus (A.D. 130), and Hippolytus (A.D. 180).

     b. The discovery of Papyrus 72, dated in the third century, shows that II Peter was well known in Egypt long before. Eusebius also states that Clement of Alexandria had II Peter in his Bible and wrote a commentary on it.

   2.   II Peter was not fully accepted into the canon of Scripture until the middle or latter part of the fourth century. Why did it take the church so long to accept II Peter as part of the canon of Scripture? This can be explained by two facts.

     a. Some letters were sent to obscure destinations and were small in content (II Peter, Jude, I, II, and III John). This kept these particular letters from becoming well-known. When they were finally circulated, the church would naturally delay in accepting them as Scripture until they could be proven to be the Word of God.

     b. Peter's name was often used to try to secure acceptance of various letters circulating at that time. The church was bound to hesitate in accepting a writing which claimed to be Peter's until proof could be secured.

   3.   Despite the questioning of the external evidence, the internal evidence favors Peter rather convincingly.

     a. The epistle says that it was written by Peter (2 Pt.1:1).

     b. The author wrote a previous epistle to the same recipients (2 Pt.3:1).

     c. The author was familiar with Paul's writings that had been sent to the same recipients (2 Pt.3:15-16). He also knew Paul rather intimately. He calls him "our beloved Paul" (2 Pt.3:15; cp. Gal.2:18f).

   4.   The author was an eyewitness of the transfiguration (2 Pt.1:16-18).

   5.   The author was aware of his pending death (2 Pt.1:13), and Peter's death was predicted by Christ (2 Pt.1:14; cp. Jn.21:18-19).

   6.   The epistle possesses no teaching that is inconsistent with the rest of Scripture. It is entirely free of personal feats to build up the author, and it is free of imaginative fables which characterized the false writings of later centuries (apocryphal books). Its content fit in much better with the early church period.

Note: the persecution that so heavily concerns First Peter had apparently now passed.

<u>**DATE**</u>: Uncertain. A.D. 61-68.

INTRODUCTION

TO WHOM WRITTEN: "To them who have obtained...faith with us" (2 Pt.1:1). "This second epistle, beloved, I now write unto you" (2 Pt.3:1).

The epistle was apparently sent to the same believers who had received I Peter. Remember: they were scattered all throughout Asia. It was also probably written from the same place, Rome. (See Introductory Notes, To Whom Written--I Peter.)

PURPOSE: To combat and warn the church against false teachers and false doctrine.

SPECIAL FEATURES:
1.   II Peter is "A General Epistle." That is, it is not written to a specific church or individual, but rather, it is written to all Christian believers.
2.   II Peter is "An Epistle Written to Combat False Teaching." From its earliest days, the church had been born in controversy.
  ⇒ At first, it was the judaizing or legalistic problem which arose at Antioch (see Acts 15:1f).
  ⇒ Then there was the denial of the literal resurrection of the body by some in the Corinthian church (1 Cor.15:1f).
  ⇒ There was also arising the corruptible beginnings of antinomianism and gnosticism. These false doctrines were appearing all throughout the Roman empire. They were using God's grace as an excuse for sinning (see Colossians, Introductory Notes, Purpose, and Master Subject Index). The epistles of II Peter, I, II, and III John, and Jude were written to combat such errors as these.
3.   II Peter is "An Epistle Stressing the Importance of Knowledge." The words *know* and *knowledge* are used about sixteen times. Knowing the truth is the answer to false teaching.
4.   II Peter is "An Epistle Verifying the Inspiration of the Scripture." Peter says "No prophecy of the Scripture is of any private interpretation [explanation or illumination]. For the prophecy came not of old time by the will of man, but holy men of God spoke as they were moved by the Holy Ghost" (2 Pt.1:20-21). Peter's statement that Paul's writings were *Scripture* shows that the canon was already being formed by the early church even while the early apostles were still alive (2 Pt.3:16; cp. 2 Tim.2:15; 3:16). The word *canon* simply means a collection of the writings considered to be inspired and breathed forth by God.
5.   II Peter is "An Epistle of the Missionary Apostle to the Jews." Peter was given the primary responsibility of reaching the circumcision throughout the world. He was the apostle to the Jews (Gal.2:7-8, 11-21). (See Author, point 10.)

THE SECOND EPISTLE GENERAL OF
PETER

CHAPTER 1

I. THE GREAT SALVATION OF GOD, 1:1-21

A. The Great Gift of Christ the Messiah: Salvation, 1:1-4

1. He is the Messiah worthy of total devotion
2. He is the Messiah of faith
   a. A most precious faith
   b. Is obtained, not earned
   c. Through the righteousness of God & Christ
3. He is the Messiah of grace & peace
   a. An abundance of both
   b. Through the knowledge of Him
4. He is the Messiah of life & godliness
   a. An abundance: All things
   b. By His divine power
   c. Through the knowledge of Him
5. He is the Messiah of the divine nature
   a. By His promises
   b. Purpose: To escape corruption

Simon Peter, a servant and an apostle of Jesus Christ, to them that have obtained like precious faith with us through the righteousness of God and our Saviour Jesus Christ:

2 Grace and peace be multiplied unto you through the knowledge of God, and of Jesus our Lord,

3 According as his divine power hath given unto us all things that pertain unto life and godliness, through the knowledge of him that hath called us to glory and virtue:

4 Whereby are given unto us exceeding great and precious promises: that by these ye might be partakers of the divine nature, having escaped the corruption that is in the world through lust.

Section I
THE GREAT SALVATION OF GOD
2 Peter 1:1-21

Study 1: **THE GREAT GIFT OF CHRIST THE MESSIAH: SALVATION**

Text: **2 Peter 1:1-4**

Aim: To sharpen your focus on the greatest gift of all--the gift of salvation.

Memory Verse:
"According as his divine power hath given unto us all things that pertain unto life and godliness, through the knowledge of him that hath called us to glory and virtue" (2 Peter 1:3).

INTRODUCTION:
Think for a moment. What is the greatest gift you have ever received? Was it...
- a brand new car?
- a large sum of money?
- an expensive antique?

We live in a world that stresses material things. Take Christmas, for example. Think how Christmas has become so commercialized. The holiday is supposed to be the celebration of the Lord's birth; but the focus of commercialism, of giving and receiving gifts, dominates the season. And often--far, far too often--the things of the world cause us to ignore the greatest gift ever given--the gift of salvation. In an attempt to put Christ back in _Christ_mas, some believers wear a button that states, *"Jesus Is The Reason For The Season."* Jesus *is* the reason for the season--but He is also the reason for *every* season of the year. Jesus Christ is your Creator and Savior, your Comforter, your Provider. And He is there for you every day of every year.

This is a great passage of Scripture. In the mind of the author, Peter, it is one of the greatest in all of Scripture. It is a passage that takes Jesus Christ and lifts Him up as the great Messiah, the Savior of the world who can meet the desperate needs of man. Here is Christ and here is the great gift of Christ the Messiah, the great gift of salvation.

OUTLINE:

1. He is the Messiah worthy of total devotion (v.1).
2. He is the Messiah of faith (v.1).
3. He is the Messiah of grace and peace (v.2).
4. He is the Messiah of life and godliness (v.3).
5. He is the Messiah of the divine nature (v.4).

1. HE IS THE MESSIAH WORTHY OF TOTAL DEVOTION (v.1).

This is seen in the two claims made by Peter.

1. *Peter calls himself the servant of Christ.* The word servant means far more than just a servant. It means a slave totally possessed by the master. It is a *bond-servant* bound by law to a master.

A look at the slave market of Peter's day shows more clearly what Peter meant when he said he was a "slave of Jesus Christ."

a. The slave was owned by his master; he was totally possessed by his master. This is what Peter meant. Peter was purchased and possessed by Christ. Christ had looked upon him and had seen his degraded and needful condition. And when Christ looked, the most wonderful thing happened: Christ *loved him and bought him*; therefore, he was now the possession of Christ.

b. The slave existed for his master and he had no other reason for existence. He had no personal rights whatsoever. The same was true with Peter: he existed only for Christ. His rights were the rights of Christ only.

c. The slave served his master and he existed only for the purpose of service. He was at the master's disposal any hour of the day. So it was with Peter: he lived only to serve Christ--hour by hour and day by day.

d. The slave's will belonged to his master. He was allowed no will and no ambition other than the will and ambition of the master. He was completely subservient to the master and owed total obedience to the will of the master. Peter belonged to Christ.

e. There is a fifth and most precious thing that Peter meant by "a slave of Jesus Christ." He meant that he had the highest and most honored and kingly profession in all the world. Men of God, the greatest men of history, have always been called *the servants of God*. It was the highest title of honor. The believer's slavery to Jesus Christ is no cringing, cowardly, shameful subjection. It is the position of honor--the honor that bestows upon a man the privileges and responsibilities of serving the King of kings and Lord of lords.

⇒ Moses was the slave of God (Dt.34:5; Ps.105:26; Mal.4:4).
⇒ Joshua was the slave of God (Josh.24:9).
⇒ David was the slave of God (2 Sam.3:18; Ps.78:70).
⇒ Peter was the slave of Jesus Christ (Ro.1:1; Ph.1:1; Tit.1:1; 2 Pt.1:1).
⇒ James was the slave of God (Jas.1:1).
⇒ Jude was the slave of God (Jude 1).
⇒ The prophets were the slaves of God (Amos 3:7; Jer.7:25).
⇒ Christian believers are said to be the slaves of Jesus Christ (Acts 2:18; 1 Cor.7:22; Eph.6:6; Col.4:12; 2 Tim.2:24).

"If any man serve me, let him follow me; and where I am, there shall also my servant be: if any man serve me, him will my Father honour" (Jn.12:26; cp. Ro.12:1; 1 Cor.15:58).

2. *Peter calls himself an apostle of Jesus Christ.* The word apostle means either a person who is sent out or a person who is sent forth. An apostle is a representative, an ambassador, a person who is sent out into one country to represent another country. Three things are true of the apostle: (1) he belongs to the One who has sent him out; (2) he is commissioned to be sent out; and (3) he possesses all the authority and power of the One who has sent him out.

Note three forceful lessons.

a. Peter said that he was *called* to be an apostle. He was not in the ministry because he...
   - chose to be.
   - had the ability.
   - had been encouraged by others to choose the *ministerial profession*.
   - enjoyed working with people.

He was an apostle, a minister of the gospel for one reason only: God had called him.

"And I thank Christ Jesus our Lord, who hath enabled me, for that he counted me faithful, putting me into the ministry" (1 Tim.1:12).

b. Peter had heard and answered God's call. God did not override Peter's will--He wanted Peter in the ministry, so He called Peter. But note: it was up to Peter to hear and respond.

c. Peter was called to be an apostle, that is, to be a minister. He was not called to occupy a position of authority or to be honored by men.

APPLICATION:

These two points stress one thing: Peter thought that Jesus Christ was worthy of total devotion. Peter made a decision to deliberately and wholly give himself to Jesus Christ. He centered his whole life around Jesus Christ. Jesus Christ was the Messiah, the Savior of the world who had been promised by God from the beginning of time, the Messiah who was worthy of total devotion.

"Then Peter began to say unto him, Lo, we have left all, and have followed thee" (Mk.10:28).

QUESTIONS:

1. Think about what Peter meant by claiming to be a servant of Jesus Christ. In that same sense, are you a true servant?
   ⇒ Are you owned and possessed by Jesus Christ.
   ⇒ Do you exist for Jesus Christ?
   ⇒ Can you honestly say you belong to Jesus Christ so wholly that His will and ambition are your will and ambition?
   ⇒ Are you proud to be a follower of Jesus Christ?
   ⇒ Are you open to God's calling in your life?
2. If you answered "No" to any of the above questions, you need to refresh your memory about who Christ is and who you are. How can you do this?

2. HE IS THE MESSIAH OF FAITH (v.1).

He is the Messiah who has made us acceptable to God by faith.

1.   The faith of Christ is a most *precious faith*. The word "precious" means of great honor and price, of great value and privilege. The faith of Jesus Christ is precious because it makes us acceptable to God. It ushers us into the very presence of God Himself.

Note this: the faith of Jesus Christ is the *same precious faith* that is given to all believers. By *precious faith* is meant *like faith*, a faith that is like everyone else's faith. This is a most wonderful thing. It means that we are all given the very same faith; we are all equal in value and honor and privilege before God. God does not discriminate; He does not have favorites. God loves us all equally and He values and honors us all as much as He did Peter and James and John and Paul.

APPLICATION:

This means that the faith of Jesus Christ eliminates prejudice and discrimination. We all stand on an equal footing before God...

- the rich and the poor
- the upper class and the lower class
- the well fed and the hungry
- the free person and the prisoner
- the religionists and the heathen
- the male and the female

If a person has obtained the precious faith of Jesus Christ, then he is acceptable to God no matter who he is. He receives the highest and most valued privilege in the whole universe: to live in the presence of God forever and ever.

2.   The faith of Jesus Christ is obtained not earned. The word "obtained" means to secure by lot; to receive by allotment; to be given a share or a portion. No person deserves the precious faith of Jesus Christ. No person can work and earn it. It is a gift of God, a free gift that is given to every person who believes in Jesus Christ.

3.   The faith of Jesus Christ comes through the righteousness of Christ. What is the righteousness of Christ? It is two things.

    a. The righteousness of Christ means that He is the righteous Man, the Perfect and Ideal Man who can stand for and cover all men. Man is not perfect, but imperfect and unrighteous. Therefore, man by his very nature cannot live in God's presence, for God is perfect and is the very embodiment of righteousness. How then can man ever become acceptable to God and be allowed to live in God's presence? Jesus Christ is the answer, for He is the righteousness of God. That is, God sent Jesus Christ to earth to live the *perfect, ideal*, and *sinless* life. Jesus Christ never sinned, not even once. Therefore, He stood before God and before the world as the Ideal Man, the Perfect Man, the Representative Man, the Perfect Righteousness that could stand for the righteousness of every man.

    When a man believes in Jesus Christ--really believes--God takes that man's faith and counts it (his faith) as righteousness. The man is not righteous; he and everyone else knows it. But God counts his faith and belief as righteousness. Why would God do such an incredible thing? Because God loves His Son that much and God loves man that much. God loves so much that He will take any man who honors His Son by believing in Him and count that man's faith as though it were the real thing: righteousness. Very simply stated: Jesus Christ is the righteousness of God. He is the only way a man can become righteous and acceptable to God.

> **"For he hath made him to be sin for us, who knew no sin; that we might be made the righteousness of God in him" (2 Cor.5:21).**

b. The righteousness of Christ means that He bore the sins of men and died for them. It is not enough for the ideal and perfect righteousness to exist, for we are already sinners. We have already transgressed God's law; we have already rebelled against God and gone our own way in life, living just like we want instead of following God. Therefore, the penalty for rebellion and treason--for sinning against God--has to be paid. We have to die or else someone else has to die for us. That someone has to be the ideal and perfect Man, for only perfection is acceptable to God. This is just what Jesus Christ did; He died for our sins. He bore the penalty and punishment for our sins. And it was acceptable to God because He was the Ideal and Perfect Man. His death stands for and covers our sins and death. Therefore, we are completely and totally free of sin. We stand before God as righteous. Now we are not righteous; we of all people know that. But God counts us free of sin--credits us as being righteous by the death of Christ.

When does God do this? When we believe in Jesus Christ. When we really believe, God counts the death of Jesus Christ *for our sins*; therefore, He is able to count us *free from sin*, as righteous before Him. This is the righteousness of Jesus Christ; this is the way we become acceptable to God.

> **"For when we were yet without strength, in due time Christ died for the ungodly" (Ro.5:6).**

QUESTIONS:
1. Who arouses faith within you? Do some believers receive more faith than others? Why or why not?
2. Can you earn faith? If not, how do you obtain it?
3. Jesus Christ is the only righteous man. He has already paid the price for your sins. Why, then, should you worry about trying to be acceptable to God?

3. HE IS THE MESSIAH OF GRACE AND PEACE (v.2).

No greater gifts exist than grace and peace. Note three things.
1.   Grace means the *undeserved favor and blessings* of God. The word *undeserved* is the key to understanding grace. Man does not deserve God's favor; he cannot earn God's approval and blessings. God is too high and man is too low for man to deserve anything from God. Man is imperfect and God is perfect; therefore, man cannot expect anything from God. Man has reacted against God too much. Man has...

- rejected God
- rebelled against God
- ignored God
- neglected God
- cursed God

- sinned against God
- disobeyed God
- denied God
- questioned God

Man deserves nothing from God except judgment, condemnation, and punishment. But God is love--perfect and absolute love. Therefore, God makes it possible for man to experience His grace, in particular the favor and blessing of salvation which is in His Son, Jesus Christ.

> **"Being justified freely by his grace through the redemption that is in Christ Jesus" (Ro.3:24).**

2.   Peace means to be bound, joined, and woven together. It also means to be bound, joined, and woven together with others and with God. It means to be assured, confident, and secure in the love and care of God. It means to have a sense, a consciousness, a knowledge that God will...

- provide
- guide
- strengthen
- sustain

- deliver
- encourage
- save
- give real life both now and forever

A person can experience true peace only as he comes to know Jesus Christ. Only Christ can bring peace to the human heart, the kind of peace that brings deliverance and assurance to the human soul.

> **"Peace I leave with you, my peace I give unto you: not as the world giveth give I unto you. Let not your heart be troubled; neither let it be afraid" (Jn.14:27).**

3.   Note that Jesus Christ multiplies grace and peace. He gives an abundance of grace and peace; He causes grace and peace to overflow in the life of the genuine believer. There is never to be a lack of grace and peace in the life of any true believer. Every believer is always to be overflowing with joy, with the favor and blessings of God, with peace in his own spirit and with God and others.

How can a person always be overflowing with the grace and peace of God? Through the knowledge of God and of Jesus our Lord. We have to know God in order to receive the grace and peace of God. What does it mean to know God? The word "knowledge" means "full, personal, precise, and correct" knowledge (The Amplified New Testament).

⇒   It means to know Christ personally; to know Him by experience. It means to know Christ just like we know any person: by walking and talking with Him.

⇒   It means to know Christ fully; to know Him in all of His person, exactly who He is. It means to be precise and correct in what we know about Him.

The point is this: if a person knows Christ fully and personally, precisely and correctly, then he knows Christ as Savior and Lord. He knows Christ as the Son of God who was sent to earth by the Father to save the world. The person does not look upon Christ as a mere man, as a great religious leader who founded the religion of Christianity. The person looks upon Jesus Christ as the Savior and Lord of men, and he knows Christ personally. He experiences Christ: he comes to Christ and asks Christ to save him and to be the Lord of his life. He gives all that he is and has to Christ, surrendering totally to Christ as his Lord. It is the person who so surrenders to Christ that comes to know Christ, and day by day, the person experiences the overflow of the Lord's grace and peace.

> **"Jesus answered them, and said, My doctrine is not mine, but his that sent me. If any man will do his will, he shall <u>know</u> of the doctrine, whether it be of God, or whether I speak of myself" (Jn.7:16-17).**

ILLUSTRATION:

When Christ fills a heart, His peace will follow. This story emphasizes this great truth.

> *"A much-beloved man, a leader in a little community of Christian students, lived such a life of serenity and peace that all his student-companions wondered. At length they determined to approach him and ask to be told the secret of his calm. They said: 'We are harassed by many temptations, which appeal to us so often and so strongly that they give us no rest. You seem to live untroubled by*

these things, and we want to know your secret. Don't the temptations that harass our souls come knocking at the door of your heart?'

"He replied: 'My children, I do know something of the things of which you speak. The temptations that trouble you do come, making their appeal to me. But when they knock at the door of my heart, I answer, 'The place is occupied.'"[1]

If you are a believer, *your place*, your heart, is also occupied by the Lord Jesus Christ.

QUESTIONS:
1. How often do you deserve God's grace? Why is grace such a need in your life?
2. What is Biblical peace? How does this kind of peace differ from the peace that the world offers? How can you have God's peace?
3. How much of your heart does Jesus occupy? What changes in your walk with the Lord need to be made to make more room for Him?

4. HE IS THE MESSIAH OF LIFE AND GODLINESS (v.3)

˒ What is meant by life and godliness? It means *all things* that are necessary for life.

First, life is the energy, the force, and the power of being. The life which Jesus Christ gives is a life of energy, force, and power.
⇒ The life given by Christ is the very opposite of perishing. It is deliverance from condemnation and death. It is the stopping or cessation of aging, deterioration, decay, and corruption. It is a life that is eternal, that lasts forever and ever. It is the very life of God Himself (Jn.17:3).
⇒ The life given by Christ is an abundant life, a life of the very highest quality, a life that overflows with all the good things of life: love, joy, peace, goodness, satisfaction, and security.

Whatever is necessary for life is given by Christ. He longs for man to live, to have an abundance of life; therefore He gives all things that will make a person overflow with life.

Second, godliness is living like God and being a godly person. It is living life like it should be lived. God gave man life; therefore, God knows what life should be, and above all things life should be godly just like God. The word "godliness" actually means to live in the reverence and awe of God; to be *so conscious* of God's presence that one lives just as God would live if He were walking upon earth. It means to live seeking to be like God; to seek to possess the very character, nature, and behavior of God. The man of God follows and runs after godliness. He seeks to gain a consciousness of God's presence--a consciousness so intense that he actually lives as God would live if He were on earth.

Note: godliness means to be *Christ-like*. Godliness is *Christ-likeness*: it is living upon earth just as Christ lived.

"But we all, with open face beholding as in a glass the glory of the Lord, are changed into the same image from glory to glory, even as by the Spirit of the Lord" (2 Cor.3:18).

Now note the verse. Two significant points are made, points that are absolutely essential for you to heed if you wish to have real life.

---

[1] *Methodist Recorder.* Walter B. Knight. *Knight's Master Book of 4,000 Illustrations.* (Grand Rapids, MI: Eerdmans Publishing Company, 1994), p.464.

1.   Note where life comes from. It does not come from man himself; life is not *in* and *of* man himself. Man dies. He is a dying creature, always in the process of dying, always moving onward toward the grave. Man is as good as dead. And in the process of dying, he experiences all kinds of trials and sufferings such as sickness, disease, accident, emptiness, loneliness, corruption, evil, shortcomings, failures, lies, thefts, killings, wars, and death after death of friends and loved ones.

Man has anything but life; at best he only exists for a few years that are ever so short and frail. Where then can man find life? Who has the power to stop the process of death and to deliver us from death? No man has such power. But note this verse: there is "divine power," the very power of Christ Himself, that can stop death and give us life-- life abundant, life now, and life eternally. Jesus Christ is the Son of God who came to earth...

- to secure the perfect and ideal life for us.
- to die for our sins in order to free us from sin so that we could stand sinless before God, perfectly righteous in the eyes of God.

This is the power of Christ, the power to save us from death and to give us life and godliness.

2.   Note how we receive life and godliness: by the knowledge of Christ. We must know Christ personally. We must know Him as our Savior and Lord, surrendering all that we are and have to him. We must be willing to walk and share with Him all day every day, serving Him as the Lord of our lives. We must be willing to know Him by living a godly life, by actually experiencing the life of God as we walk day by day.

Note: Christ has called us to a life of glory and moral excellence both here on this earth and in heaven. We are to live pure and righteous lives, glorious lives; and when we do, He promises to give us a place in the glory and perfection of heaven.

> **"Verily, verily, I say unto you, He that heareth my Word, and believeth on him that sent me, hath everlasting life, and shall not come into condemnation; but is passed from death unto life"** (Jn.5:24).

QUESTIONS:
1. Life. Who gave it to you? Can man create what God has given you? Eternal life? A life free from perishing?
2. Considering what Christ has given you, you should want to be like Him, that is, Christ-like. How can you achieve this?
3. Is it sufficient just to know *about* Christ? What does God expect you to do in your Christian walk day by day?

5. HE IS THE MESSIAH OF THE DIVINE NATURE (v.4).

Note: exceeding great and precious promises have been given to us. The promises are those that have to do with the *divine nature* of God, the divine nature that is planted within the heart of a person who believes in Jesus Christ. When a person believes in Jesus Christ, God sends His Spirit, the Holy Spirit, to indwell the heart of the believer. God places within the heart of the believer His own divine nature and makes him a new creature and a new man. The believer is actually *born again* spiritually. He actually partakes of the divine nature of God through the presence of God's Holy Spirit.

And note what happens: the believer escapes the corruption that is in the world. He lives eternally, for the divine nature of God can never die. When it is time for the believer to depart this life, quicker than the blink of an eye, his spirit is transferred into heaven, into the very presence of God Himself. Why? Because of the divine presence of God: the believer is a new creature, a new man, a person in whom the very Spirit of God

Himself dwells; and the Spirit of God cannot die. The person thereby escapes the corruption of this world. (See **A CLOSER LOOK**, <u>Corruption</u>--2 Pt.1:4 for more discussion.)

$\Rightarrow$ The believer is born again.

> **"Jesus answered and said unto him, Verily, verily, I say unto thee, Except a man be born again, he cannot see the kingdom of God. Nicodemus saith unto him, How can a man be born when he is old? can he enter the second time into his mother's womb, and be born? Jesus answered, Verily, verily, I say unto thee, Except a man be born of water and of the Spirit, he cannot enter into the kingdom of God. That which is born of the flesh is flesh; and that which is born of the Spirit is spirit" (Jn.3:3-6).**

$\Rightarrow$ The believer is made into a new creature.

> **"Therefore if any man be in Christ, he is a new creature: old things are passed away; behold, all things are become new" (2 Cor.5:17).**

$\Rightarrow$ The believer is made into a new man.

> **"And that ye put on the new man, which after God is created in righteousness and true holiness" (Eph.4:24).**

$\Rightarrow$ The believer is given the divine nature of God.

> **"Whereby are given unto us exceeding great and precious promises: that by these ye might be partakers of the divine nature, having escaped the corruption that is in the world through lust" (2 Pt.1:4).**

ILLUSTRATION:
When we are born again we leave behind the corruption that devastated our souls. This corruption is not just in those who came out of the dark gutters. It applies to everyone--even you.

> *"In England there is a paper factory that makes the finest stationery in the world. One day a man touring the factory asked what it [the stationery] was made from. He was shown a huge pile of old rags and told that the rag content was what determined the quality of the paper. The visitor wouldn't believe it. In weeks he received from the company a package of paper with his initials embossed on it. On the top piece were written the words 'Dirty rags transformed.'*
> *"The same is true of the Christian life. It is a process of transformation from what we were into something new and wonderful."* [2]

> **"But we are all as an unclean *thing*, and all <u>our righteousnesses</u> <u>*are* as filthy rags</u>; and we all do fade as a leaf; and our iniquities, like the wind, have taken us away" (Is.64:6).**

Being born again is the soul's only remedy for the lethal poison of corruption.

---

[2] Michael P. Green. *Illustrations for Biblical Preaching*. (Grand Rapids, MI: Baker Books, 1996), p.81.

A CLOSER LOOK:

(1:4) **Corruption**: the body of man has within it the principle or the seed of corruption, and the world in which man lives has within it the principle or the seed of corruption. Therefore, man deteriorates and decays--he dies and returns to dust.

This seed of corruption is caused by sin. Sin is selfishness or lust. Sin is acting against God, against others, and even against oneself.

When a man offends--when he acts selfishly, does what he wants instead of what he should do--when he acts *against* instead of *for*--he energizes and sets in motion the process of corruption. Man's selfishness corrupts himself and the world in which he lives-- including the ground, the air, and the water of the earth (Ro.8:21). His selfishness corrupts the relationship between himself and God, between himself and other persons, and even the relationship between other persons. His selfishness and sin corrupt his own body (1 Cor.15:42). It may be nothing more than eating too much or failing to stay physically fit, but his selfishness and sin set in motion the process of corruption. And the process of corruption just continues and continues to eat away at life. Sin, that is, selfishness, has caused and is causing death, both physically and spiritually.

SUMMARY:

God did not hold back anything when we needed His very best. Without hesitation, God sent His Son into the world. If you are ever tempted to ask God to prove His love to you, look no further than Jesus Christ.

Jesus Christ is the greatest gift that has ever been given. What makes Him such a precious treasure?

1. He is the Messiah worthy of total devotion.
2. He is the Messiah of faith.
3. He is the Messiah of grace and peace.
4. He is the Messiah of life and godliness.
5. He is the Messiah of the divine nature.

2 PETER 1:1-4

PERSONAL JOURNAL NOTES:
(Reflection & Response)

1. The most important thing that I learned from this lesson was:

2. The thing that I need to work on the most is:

3. I can apply this lesson to my life by:

4. Closing Prayer of Commitment: (put your commitment down on paper).

1. The charge to add "these things"

a. Add virtue
b. Add knowledge
c. Add temperance or self-control
d. Add patience
e. Add godliness

f. Add brotherly kindness
g. Add love

2. The great power of "these things"

a. These things keep you from being barren or unfruitful

b. These things keep you from being spiritually blind

c. These things keep you from forgetting that you have been cleansed from your sins

B. The Great Things of the Believer's Life, 1:5-15

5 And beside this, giving all diligence, add to your faith virtue; and to virtue knowledge;
6 And to knowledge temperance; and to temperance patience; and to patience godliness;
7 And to godliness brotherly kindness; and to brotherly kindness charity.
8 For if these things be in you, and abound, they make you that ye shall neither be barren nor unfruitful in the knowledge of our Lord Jesus Christ.
9 But he that lacketh these things is blind, and cannot see afar off, and hath forgotten that he was purged from his old sins.
10 Wherefore the rather, brethren, give diligence to make your calling and election sure: for if ye do these things, ye shall never fall:
11 For so an entrance shall be ministered unto you abundantly into the everlasting kingdom of our Lord and Saviour Jesus Christ.
12 Wherefore I will not be negligent to put you always in remembrance of these things, though ye know them, and be established in the present truth.
13 Yea, I think it meet, as long as I am in this tabernacle, to stir you up by putting you in remembrance;
14 Knowing that shortly I must put off this my tabernacle, even as our Lord Jesus Christ hath showed me.
15 Moreover I will endeavor that ye may be able after my decease to have these things always in remembrance.

d. These things keep you from falling

e. These things give you eternal life & more

3. The great importance of "these things"

a. To always preach these things
   1) Not to neglect them
   2) To preach them although believers are grounded therein

b. To always stir believers about these things, as long as you are alive

c. To see that believers are stirred over these things even after your death
   1) To die soon
   2) To have a lasting ministry is essential

Section I
THE GREAT SALVATION OF GOD
2 Peter 1:1-21

Study 2: **THE GREAT THINGS OF THE BELIEVER'S LIFE**

Text: **2 Peter 1:5-15**

Aim: To instill within yourself the great virtues of the believer's life.

Memory Verse:

> "For if these things be in you, and abound, they make you that ye shall neither be barren nor unfruitful in the knowledge of our Lord Jesus Christ" (2 Peter 1:8).

INTRODUCTION:

Anyone who has driven a car knows that you must add certain things to keep it operating. If you do not add things like gas and oil for the engine and air for the tires when needed, the car will be useless. All of this makes sense, and yet every day someone...

- runs out of gas
- forgets to put oil in the engine
- neglects to keep the necessary amount of air in the tires

Common sense tells us that whether the car is brand new from the showroom or a rattletrap held together with bailing wire, these things must be added on a regular basis. This same principle holds true for the Christian believer. You can be a brand new convert or a saint who has walked with Christ for many years--the need remains the same. Every Christian needs to add "these things" that Peter will be discussing. If you neglect to add these things, you will find yourself doing what the neglected car does: running out of gas, blowing off steam, and breaking down--far away from the One who can help you!

This is one of the most important passages in all of Scripture for the believer, a passage that must be studied and heeded time and again. It covers the great things (qualities and virtues) which are to be in the life of the believer. The great importance of "these things" is seen in three facts that are forcefully stressed by Peter.

First, a person is to give *all diligence*, to add "these things" to his faith and life. As Scripture says, the believer "is to work out his own salvation" (Ph.2:12).

Second, the *great power* of "these things" stresses their importance. *These things* work within the life of the believer to meet five desperate needs of man, five things for which the soul of the believer aches and longs. Glancing at the five points of verses 8-11 in the outline of the Scripture will again show the great importance of these things in the believer's life.

Third, Peter's heavy stress upon the importance of "these things" is phenomenal.

⇒ Note v.12: Peter says that he is going to always preach *these things* despite the fact that the believer already knows them. But this is not all.

⇒ Note v.13: Peter says that as long as he is living, he is going to stir up the believers by reminding them of *these things*. But this is not all.

⇒ Note v.14-15: Peter says that *these things* are so important that he is going to see to it that the believers are reminded of them *even after his death*.

What more could Peter say?

OUTLINE:

1. The charge to add *these things* (v.5-7).
2. The great power of *these things* (v.8-11).
3. The great importance of *these things* (v.12-15).

1. THE CHARGE TO ADD "THESE THINGS" (v.5-7).

To "add" here means in addition to God's great salvation--right along side of what God has done--add *these things*. And give *all diligence* to adding them. Hasten, jump, act now to add them; don't wait. Be energetic and earnest; strenuously work to add *these things* to your faith and salvation.

1. Add "virtue": moral excellence and goodness of character; moral strength and moral courage. It means manliness; being an excellent person in life, a real man or a real

woman in life; living life just like one should, in the most excellent way. It means always choosing the excellent way.

> **"Furthermore then we beseech you, brethren, and exhort you by the Lord Jesus, that as ye have received of us how ye ought to walk and to please God, so ye would abound more and more. For ye know what commandments we gave you by the Lord Jesus. For this is the will of God, even your sanctification, that ye should abstain from fornication: that every one of you should know how to possess his vessel in sanctification and honour; not in the lust of concupiscence [evil passion], even as the Gentiles which know not God: that no man go beyond and defraud his brother in any matter: because that the Lord is the avenger of all such, as we also have forewarned you and testified. For God hath not called us unto uncleanness, but unto holiness"** (1 Th.4:1-7).

2.   Add "knowledge": practical intelligence, practical knowledge, practical insight. It means knowing what to do in every situation and doing it; it is practical, day to day knowledge that sees situations and knows how to handle them. It is seeing the trials and temptations of life and knowing what to do with them and doing it.

Remember the charge: we must add knowledge to our faith. We must give diligent attention to the situations of life and figure out how to conquer them.

> **"Then said Jesus to those Jews which believed on him, If ye continue in my word, then are ye my disciples indeed"** (Jn.8:31).

3.   Add "temperance": to master and control the body or the flesh with all of its lusts. It means self-control, the master of desire, appetite and passion, especially sensual urges and cravings. It means to be strong and controlled and restrained. It means to stand against the lust of the flesh and the lust of the eye and the pride of life (1 Jn.2:15-16).

⇒   The believer is to know that self-control is of God, a fruit of the Holy Spirit.

> **"But the fruit of the Spirit is love, joy, peace, longsuffering, gentleness, goodness, faith, meekness, <u>temperance</u>: against such there is no law"** (Gal.5:22-23).

⇒   The believer is to proclaim self-control to the lost.

> **"And as he reasoned of righteousness, <u>temperance</u>, and judgment to come, Felix trembled, and answered, Go thy way for this time; when I have a convenient season, I will call for thee"** (Acts 24:25).

⇒   The believer is to control his sexual desires.

> **"But if they cannot contain [control], let them marry: for it is better to marry than to burn"** (1 Cor.7:9).

⇒   The believer is to strenuously exercise self-control, just as an athlete controls himself.

> **"And every man that striveth for the mastery is temperate in all things. Now they do it to obtain a corruptible crown; but we an incorruptible" (1 Cor.9:25).**

⇒ The believer is to grow in self-control.

> **"And to knowledge <u>temperance</u>; and to temperance patience; and to patience godliness" (2 Pt.1:6).**

⇒ The aged believer is especially to be on guard to control himself.

> **"That the aged men be sober, grave, temperate, sound in faith, in charity, in patience" (Tit.2:2).**

4.   Add "patience": endurance, fortitude, stedfastness, constancy, perseverance. The word is not passive; it is active. It is not the spirit that just sits back and puts up with the trials of life, taking whatever may come. Rather it is the spirit that stands up and faces life's trials, that actively goes about conquering and overcoming them. When trials confront a man who is truly justified, he is stirred to arise and face the trials head on. He immediately sets out to conquer and overcome them. He knows that God is allowing the trials in order to teach him more and more patience (endurance).

> **"For ye have need of patience, that, after ye have done the will of God, ye might receive the promise" (Heb.10:36).**

QUESTIONS:
1. How hard do you really try to add "these things" to your life?
   ⇒ Virtue?
   ⇒ Knowledge?
   ⇒ Self-control?
   ⇒ Patience?
   ⇒ Brotherly love?
   ⇒ Kindness?
Can you do even better? In what practical ways?
2. How would your life differ if these qualities were a stronger part of your character?

5.   Add "godliness": see 2 Pt.1:3 for discussion.
6.   Add "brotherly kindness": the very special love that exists between brothers and sisters within a loving family, brothers and sisters who truly cherish one another. It is the kind of love...
- that binds people together as a family, as a brotherly clan.
- that binds people in an unbreakable union.
- that holds people ever so dearly within the heart.
- that knows deep affection for other people.
- that nourishes and nurtures other people.
- that shows concern and looks after the welfare of other people.
- that joins hands with other people in a common purpose *under one father.*[1]

How can people possibly love one another like this when they are not true blood brothers and sisters? Here is how. The Greek word "brother" means *from the same womb.* The

---

[1]   Leon Morris. *The Epistles of Paul to the Thessalonians.* "Tyndale New Testament Commentary," Ed. by RVG Tasker. (Grand Rapids, MI: Eerdmans Publishing Company, 1956), p.80.

word used for love is phileo which means deep-seated affection and care, deep and warm feelings within the heart. It is the kind of love that holds a person near and dear to one's heart. Now note: the two Greek words are combined together by the writer to convey what he means by *brotherly love*.

⇒ People who have *brotherly love* have come from the same womb, that is, from the same source. They have been *born again* by the Spirit of God through faith in the Lord Jesus Christ. When they receive this new birth, God gives them a new spirit--a spirit that melts and binds their hearts and lives in love for all the family of God.

Believers may not even know each other. They may even be from different parts of the world, but there is a *brotherly love* between them because they have been given a new birth and a new spirit of love by God. They are brothers and sisters in the family of God--the family of those who truly believe in God's Son, the Lord Jesus Christ--the family who has received a new spirit that binds them together in brotherly love. This new spirit, of course, comes from the Holy Spirit of God Himself.

> **"A new commandment I give unto you, That ye love one another; as I have loved you, that ye also love one another. By this shall all men know that ye are my disciples, if ye have love one to another" (Jn.13:34-35).**

7.   Add "love": the love of the mind, of the reason, of the will. It is the *agape love* of God, the love that goes so far...

- that it loves regardless of feelings--whether a person feels like loving or not.
- that it loves a person even if the person does not deserve to be loved.
- that it actually loves the person who is utterly unworthy of being loved.

Note four significant points about *agape love*.

a. Selfless or agape love is the love of God, the very love possessed by God Himself. It is the love demonstrated in the cross of Christ.

⇒ It is the love of God for the *ungodly*.

> **"For when we were yet without strength, in due time Christ died for the ungodly" (Ro.5:6).**

⇒ It is the love of God for *unworthy sinners*.

> **"But God commendeth his love toward us, in that, while we were yet sinners, Christ died for us" (Ro.5:8).**

⇒ It is the love of God for *undeserving enemies*.

> **"For if, when we were enemies, we were reconciled to God by the death of his Son, much more, being reconciled, we shall be saved by his life" (Ro.5:10).**

b. Selfless or agape love is a gift of God. It can be experienced only if a person knows God *personally*--only if a person has received the love of God, that is, Christ Jesus, into his heart and life. *Agape love* has to be shed abroad (poured out, flooded, spread about) by the Spirit of God within the heart of a person.

> **"And hope maketh not ashamed; because the love of God is shed abroad in our hearts by the Holy Ghost which is given unto us" (Ro.5:5).**

c. Selfless or agape love is the greatest thing in all of life according to the Lord Jesus Christ.

> "And Jesus answered him, The <u>first of all the commandments</u> is, Hear, O Israel; The Lord our God is one Lord: and thou shalt love the Lord thy God with all thy heart, and with all thy soul, and with all thy mind, and with all thy strength: this is the <u>first commandment</u>. And the second is like, namely this, Thou shalt love thy neighbor as thyself. There is <u>none other commandment</u> greater than these" (Mk.12:29-31).

d. Selfless or agape love is the greatest possession and gift in human life according to the Scripture (1 Cor.13:1-13).

> "And now abideth faith, hope, charity [love], these three; but the greatest of these is charity" (1 Cor.13:13).

ILLUSTRATION:
Who can fully explain the power of agape love--the love that gives so much to those it touches? God's kind of love opens a heart that has been nailed shut by sin.

> *"After the U.S.S. Pueblo was captured by the North Koreans, the eighty-two surviving crew members were thrown into a brutal captivity. In one particular instance thirteen of the men were required to sit in a rigid manner around a table for hours. After several hours the door was violently flung open and a North Korean guard brutally beat the man in the first chair with the butt of his rifle. The next day, as each man sat at his assigned place, again the door was thrown open and the man in the first chair was brutally beaten. On the third day it happened again to the same man. Knowing the man could not survive, another young sailor took his place. When the door was flung open the guard automatically beat the new victim senseless. For weeks, each day a new man stepped forward to sit in that horrible chair, knowing full well what would happen. At last the guards gave up in exasperation. They were unable to beat that kind of sacrificial love."[2]*

How far would you be willing to go--in the name of love?

QUESTIONS:
1. What is so unique about brotherly kindness? Do you *feel* loved when you are among fellow believers? Do you *show* love?
2. Agape love is different from brotherly kindness. How can you show agape love for the 'unlovable'? And why should you?

2. THE GREAT POWER OF "THESE THINGS" (v.8-11).

Note how the great needs of man's heart and life are covered in these verses:
⇒ Man is barren and unfruitful in life (v.8).
⇒ Man is blind, cannot see the purpose, meaning, and significance of life and cannot see how to be absolutely sure of tomorrow, much less the distant future (v.9).
⇒ Man forgets, does not know how to deal with sin. Or if he knows how--knows the gospel--he is unwilling to give up his sin (v.9).

---

[2] Michael P. Green. *Illustrations for Biblical Preaching*, p.226-227.

⇒ Man does not know how to keep from falling in life, from failing and coming short. He does not know how to meet his full potential; how to control the problems of life, to bring love, peace, and joy to himself and his loved ones and the world (v.10).

⇒ Man does not know how to gain and be perfectly assured of eternal life; he does not know how to receive an abundant entrance into the everlasting kingdom of Christ (v.11).

But note: all these needs can be met perfectly. They are met if *these things* of verses 7-8 are added to our lives in abundance. The word "abound" means to increase and grow; to overflow and be filled with more and more, ever learning how to increase these things in our lives. In other words, do not be satisfied...

- with your life as it is.
- with present growth.
- with staying where you are spiritually.
- with just knowing Jesus.
- with doing no more than what you are currently doing.

To have the needs of our hearts and lives met, we must continue on in *these things*. We have to grow and grow in them; give them utmost attention; go after them ever so diligently, never slackening. If we abound in them, then the needs of our hearts and lives will be met to the fullest.

1. We will not be *barren nor unfruitful*.

⇒ The word barren means idle and slothful; being empty and useless. It is the very opposite of being fruitful and productive in life. Therefore if we do *these things*, if we really work at our salvation, we will not live a barren, dry life. We will not be unfruitful nor live a life that is empty and useless, idle and slothful. On the contrary, we will live a life that flows with nourishment and that bears the ripest fruit: love, joy, and peace (cp. Gal.5:22-23).

But note the source of such a life: the source is our Lord Jesus Christ. We must know Him and grow in the knowledge of Him. The knowledge of Him must be our aim and purpose in life. Only as we know Him can we overcome the barrenness and unfruitfulness of life. He and He alone can give us real life. Therefore, we must do *these things*--really work at our salvation, really seek fellowship and communion with Christ moment by moment and day by day--in order not to be barren or unfruitful in the knowledge of Him. We must learn to pray all day long and to take *set times* for prayer every day, set times for concentrated prayer. We must learn to *keep our minds* on Christ.

> "I am the vine, ye are the branches: He that <u>abideth</u> in me, and I in him, the same bringeth forth much fruit: for without me ye can do nothing. If a man abide not in me, he is cast forth as a branch, and is withered; and men gather them, and cast them into the fire, and they are burned" (Jn.15:5-6).

2. We will not be *blind and shortsighted*. Without Christ men are blind. They do not see...

- the purpose, meaning, or significance to life.
- the importance of morality, virtue, love, joy, peace, and the goodness of God and Christ.
- the way to conquer sin and evil, trials and suffering, life and death.

Men are pictured as being unable to see afar off, as being short-sighted. They are pictured as keeping their eyes only on the earth and its pleasures and possessions, only upon enjoying life now, only upon living as they want and doing their own thing. They give little if any thought to the *eternal consequences* of their behavior and actions. The result is devastating: they are blind and shortsighted. They lack real and permanent purpose, meaning, and significance in life. They experience ever so much emptiness and loneliness, often wondering...

- what is life all about?
- what is its purpose and end?
- what is there after death?
- is there meaning to this life at all?

But note: if we do *these things*, if we work at our salvation, we will not be blind or unable to see ahead. We will not lack purpose, meaning, or significance in life. *These things*, the things of salvation, will not only give us purpose in this life, they will give us eternal purpose. We will understand life, what life is all about. We will know the purpose, meaning, and significance of life. We will never be empty or lonely, or without purpose in life.

> **"But if thine eye be evil, thy whole body shall be full of darkness. If therefore the light that is in thee be darkness, how great is that darkness!" (Mt.6:23).**

3. We will not *forget that we have been cleansed from our sins*. Very frankly, the person who fails to do *these things*, who fails to work out his own salvation, soon forgets the death of Christ. He forgets the great price that Christ paid to forgive his sins. The person becomes a backslider. How can we say this? Because a person is either moving ahead in Christ or else sliding back from Christ. And the person sliding back thinks little about sin and the consequences of sin. His thoughts and actions are in the world, and he is focusing upon the world and its pleasures and possessions. He has just forgotten that Christ purged him from his sins. He has slipped away from Christ and slipped back into the world.

The point is this: we must do *these things*, work out our own salvation, or else we will backslide. We will forget Christ and His death and the glorious fact that He has forgiven our sins. *These things*, the wonderful things of salvation, have the power to keep us near Christ and to keep us from ever backsliding.

> **"But now, after that ye have known God, or rather are known of God, how turn ye again to the weak and beggarly elements?" (Gal.4:9).**

4. We will *never fall*. How often we come short, stumble, and fall. We just do not do what we should. If there is any single trait that runs through human life, it is stumbling, coming short, and falling. People stumble, come short, and fall...

- in devotions
- in witnessing
- in serving Christ
- in worship
- in marriage
- in family duties
- in relationships
- in work
- in school
- in responsibilities
- in life
- in promises
- in planning
- in behavior
- in resolutions
- in Christian life

How can we keep from stumbling and falling? God has called and elected us to live a rich, fruitful life, to be rich and fruitful for all eternity. How can we live such a rich, fruitful life? Note the verse:

> **"Give diligence to make your calling and election sure: for if ye do these things, ye shall never fall" (v.10).**

We must be diligent in doing *these things*. We must give ourselves totally to the things of salvation. We must work and work at them. If we do, then we shall never stumble and fall, not in a tragic, devastating, or destructive sense. On the contrary, we will live the most abundant and fruitful life imaginable.

> "Therefore, my beloved brethren, be ye stedfast, unmoveable,
> always abounding in the work of the Lord, forasmuch as ye know
> that your labor is not in vain in the Lord" (1 Cor.15:58).

5.   We will be given *eternal life and more*. We will receive an abundant entrance into the kingdom of our Lord and Savior Jesus Christ. The word *abundant* means rich. We will be richly and gloriously welcomed into heaven. The idea is that there will be different degrees of reward, of richness and wealth in heaven. Some of us will not inherit the kingdom, wealth, and service that others will inherit. How can we be sure of receiving the richest entrance into heaven? By being diligent in doing *these things*, in working out our salvation.

> "Then shall the King say unto them on his right hand, Come, ye
> blessed of my Father, inherit the kingdom prepared for you from
> the foundation of the world: for I was an hungered, and ye gave me
> meat: I was thirsty, and ye gave me drink: I was a stranger, and ye
> took me in: naked, and ye clothed me: I was sick, and ye visited me:
> I was in prison, and ye came unto me" (Mt.25:34-36).

3. THE GREAT IMPORTANCE OF "THESE THINGS" (v.12-15).

What Peter does now is most interesting. He tells us how important he considers these things.
1.   They are so important that he is always going to preach and teach these things. He is going to continually remind believers of them. Genuine believers know them and are even established in *these things*. But Peter says he is going to persist in repeating them. He will not neglect them.
One thing is sure: Peter thought that *these things*, the things of salvation, were essential. How much more should we stress them! But note the next point. Peter has even more to say about *these things*.
2.   They are so important that he is going to stir believers to do them as long as he is alive. He is going to continually remind them of these things as long as he is in "this tabernacle," the tent of his body. Peter has to persist in repeating these things. Why? Because it is right, the only right thing to do. Believers must do *these things* in order to experience the rich and fruitful life Christ gives. Therefore, he must stress them and drive them home to the hearts of his dear people. But note: this is still not all Peter has to say about *these things*.
3.   They are so important that Peter is going to see that believers are stirred to do *these things* even after his death. Peter apparently knew he was soon to be taken on home to heaven. But *these things* were so important he was going to make arrangements with those left behind to teach *these things*.

APPLICATION:
How important are *these things*? How important is it that we preach and teach *these things*? Few Scriptures are stressed and emphasized as much as these. Peter said an astounding thing, that he was going to see to it these things were taught to believers. He said this three times. This alone should stir us to preach and teach them--always--ever so diligently and faithfully.

"**And he said unto them, Go ye into all the world, and preach the gospel to every creature**" (Mk.16:15).

ILLUSTRATION:

When you leave this earth, what will be said about you? What kind of legacy will you leave behind? Every believer has the opportunity to leave behind a great legacy. A man named Bob lost his battle with cancer but he won the war.

Bob was a believer who made it his life's task to memorize God's Word and live by it. He was known by many as the walking Bible concordance. Being full of God's Word, Bob never lacked a good word for anybody who needed encouragement or hope. Bob took to heart this Psalm:

"**Thy word have I hid in mine heart, that I might not sin against thee**" (Ps.119:11).

What did Bob leave behind? Many men whom he discipled caught the purpose of Bob's life--to memorize and live out the Word of God. Our greatest legacy is in the people we leave behind. What will be *your* legacy?

QUESTIONS:

1. Are you disciplined enough to keep on for Christ, to keep stressing virtue, knowledge, self-control, patience, godliness, brotherly kindness, and love? What will improve your discipline?
2. Whom do you have an impact upon in your day to day walk? Name a few people. Are you influencing them for Christ? Sharing Christ with them? What kind of impact are you making?
3. What will be your legacy? How will this be determined?
4. If the Lord tarries, what kind of impact will your life make five years from now? Twenty years? One hundred years?

SUMMARY:

The challenge to believers is to do *something* with *these things:* virtue, knowledge, self-control, patience, godliness, brotherly kindness, and love. If Jesus came back today, would you be found faithful to these things? It is essential--absolutely essential--that you make these things a vital part of your life. In this portion of Scripture, you have been given these reminders:

1. The charge to add *these things*.
2. The great power of *these things*.
3. The great importance of *these things*.

2 PETER 1:5-15

PERSONAL JOURNAL NOTES:
(Reflection & Response)

1. The most important thing that I learned from this lesson was:

2. The thing that I need to work on the most is:

3. I can apply this lesson to my life by:

4. Closing Prayer of Commitment: (put your commitment down on paper).

	C. The Great Proof of Salvation, 1:16-21	heard, when we were with him in the holy mount.	
1. The great truth: Salvation is not a fable; it is the power and coming of Christ	16 For we have not followed cunningly devised fables, when we made known unto you the power and coming of our Lord Jesus Christ, but were eyewitnesses of his majesty.	19 We have also a more sure word of prophecy; whereunto ye do well that ye take heed, as unto a light that shineth in a dark place, until the day dawn, and the day star arise in your hearts:	3. The second proof of salvation: Scripture—the more sure account of prophecy or Scripture
2. The first proof of salvation: The great eyewitness account of Christ's majesty & transfiguration			a. Scripture is more sure than an eyewitness account
a. The honor & glory of God	17 For he received from God the Father honour and glory, when there came such a voice to him from the excellent glory, This is my beloved Son, in whom I am well pleased.	20 Knowing this first, that no prophecy of the scripture is of any private interpretation.	b. Scripture is to be heeded
b. The voice from heaven			c. Scripture is not of private interpretation
		21 For the prophecy came not in old time by the will of man: but holy men of God spake as they were moved by the Holy Ghost.	1) Because it is not given by man's will
c. The testimony: "We heard"	18 And this voice which came from heaven we		2) Because it is given by the Spirit

Section I
THE GREAT SALVATION OF GOD
2 Peter 1:1-21

Study 3: **THE GREAT PROOF OF SALVATION**

Text: **2 Peter 1:16-21**

Aim: To understand and testify to the great proof of salvation.

Memory Verse:
> "We have also a more sure word of prophecy; whereunto ye take heed, as unto a light that shineth in a dark place, until the day dawn, and the day star arise in your hearts" (2 Peter 1:19).

INTRODUCTION:

If you were put on trial for being a Christian, would there be enough evidence to convict you? Think about it. What proof would you be able to offer the skeptic in order to validate your salvation?

⇒ Would your Christian heritage be convincing to a jury?
⇒ Would your good deeds make the difference?
⇒ Would your keeping the law prove your claim?

Contrary to popular opinion, these things do not make a person a Christian believer. If not these things, then what does?

How do we know that we can really be saved? That the glorious gospel of salvation is true? How do we know that Jesus Christ is really the Son of God, the Messiah and Savior of the world? This is the subject of this great passage--*the great proof of salvation.*

OUTLINE:

1. The great truth: salvation is not a fable; it is the power and coming of Christ (v.16).
2. The first proof of salvation: the great eyewitness account of Christ's majesty and transfiguration (v.16-18).
3. The second proof of salvation: Scripture--the more sure account of prophecy or Scripture (v.19-21).

1. THE GREAT TRUTH: SALVATION IS NOT A FABLE; IT IS THE POWER AND COMING OF CHRIST (v.16).

1. The word *fable* is described as *a cunningly devised fable*. The gospel of salvation is not a story, some fictitious creation of man's mind. It is not an invention of man's imagination. It has not been thought up in order to give man more...

- peace
- security
- peace
- love
- joy
- morality
- goodness
- righteousness
- justice
- life

Man has created great value systems, religions, and laws to meet his need for peace, security, hope, and life. Some persons even declare that science and technology, education and social services are the answer to meeting man's needs. They think through the problems of life, and with great creative imagination they work out how technology and education can meet these needs. They then put their thoughts in writing and declare to the world that the salvation of man is found in technology and education. They declare that the needs of man for peace, security, and life are found in the works of man's own hands...

- in human religion and value systems
- in human laws and good behavior
- in science and technology
- in education and social services

But note: there is one terrible flaw in all this. Nothing on this earth is permanent; nothing lasts, not beyond this life. The cry of man's heart is for life, for fulness of life, for completeness, fulfillment, and satisfaction. Man longs for life, for security, hope, assurance, and peace. Man cries out for an abundance of life both now and in the future, life in this world and in the next world. In addition to the cry for life, man has a spiritual sense of God and of living forever, the need to worship God and to live with Him forever. But man dies and leaves this world. If he depends upon his own man-made efforts to meet his needs, then his efforts die when he dies. Why? Because no man can give him life beyond the grave. He depends upon his own mind and hands to make him secure in the future and in the hereafter, but when his mind and hands die, they are dead. His mind and hands cannot deliver him; they are lifeless and powerless.

This means something: all the man-made efforts to save man, all the creations of man's mind and hands that claim to be the salvation of man, are all fabrications of the human mind. They are the real *cunningly devised fables*. They may be helpful to man; they may meet some needs to some degree. In fact, all great thoughts and acts of men do help to some degree. But no thought of man and no act of man can meet the needs of man, *not perfectly and not eternally*. For all men die. In just a few short years there will not be a single person alive who is living upon the earth today--not a single person. We shall all be gone forever, never to return. No matter how great a thought we think and no matter how great a human salvation we make with our hands, we shall be gone forever. If we are going to meet our needs for life, if we are going to live abundantly both now and in the other world (heaven), then God Himself has to show us how to live and how to get into the other world. God Himself has to show us how to please Him so that He will take us there.

Note: if there is a God in another world, in a spiritual dimension, who has made us and the world, then He is interested in our getting to where He is. He is interested in our living with Him. There is too much good and love within the world and too much longing for Him and for life eternal within us for God not to love us. And this is the glorious gospel: God does love us. He has not left us in the dark to grope and grasp after Him. He has revealed Himself and shown us how to reach and please Him. He has shown us how to be acceptable to Him and to receive eternal life. The gospel of salvation is not a fable; it is not a cunning device of man's imagination that deceives people. It is the truth that God loves us and has provided a way for us to be saved, a way for us to have peace and life now while on this earth and eternally when we enter the next world.

> **"Beware of false prophets, which come to you in sheep's cloth-
> ing, but inwardly they are ravening wolves" (Mt.7:15).**

ILLUSTRATION:
What kind of Savior do you need? In a lost and dying world, He must be all-powerful. Listen to these comments.

> *"This story is told of Daniel Webster when he was in the prime of his man-
> hood. He was dining in the company of literary men in Boston. During the din-
> ner the conversation turned upon the subject of Christianity. Mr. Webster frankly
> stated his belief in the divinity of Christ and his dependence upon the atonement
> of the Saviour.*
> *"One said to him, 'Mr. Webster, can you comprehend how Christ could be
> both God and man?' Mr. Webster promptly replied, 'No, sir, I cannot compre-
> hend it. If I could comprehend him, he would be no greater than myself. I feel
> that I need a super-human Saviour.'"*[1]

Is your God small enough to comprehend? Like Webster, we all need a "super-human Savior!"

2. Salvation is the power and coming of our Lord Jesus Christ. What does this mean?
   a. First, it means the first coming of Jesus Christ. God has not left man in the dark to seek and search for peace and life--to see if there is such a thing as absolute peace of heart and such a thing as real life both now and hereafter. Only a *God of hate* would leave man in the dark to grasp after the truth within a corruptible world. But this is not God, not the true and living God. God is love and He cares deeply for man.
   ⇒ The fact that God sent Christ into the world to save us means that God loves us and has the power to save us. God loves us enough and has enough power to give us peace and life both now and eternally. The power and coming of Jesus Christ into the world proves this.

> **"For God so loved the world, that he gave his only be-
> gotten Son, that whosoever believeth in him should not per-**

---

[1] *Christian Witness.* Paul Lee Tan. *Encyclopedia of 7,700 Illustrations: Signs of the Times.* (Rockville, MD: Assurance Publishers, 1985), p.649.

ish, but have everlasting life. For God sent not his Son into the world to condemn the world; but that the world through him might be saved" (Jn.3:16-17).

b. Second, it means the second coming of Christ. God is going to reveal His love and power again; God is going to prove His power to give us peace and life by sending Christ back to earth. Jesus Christ is going to come again just as He came before. Note the verse: this is not a "cunningly devised fable...the power and coming of our Lord Jesus Christ." God has the power to bring peace to this earth, and He is going to personally come to earth to bring peace to it. He is coming again in the person of His Son Jesus Christ.

"For as the lightning cometh out of the east, and shineth even unto the west; so shall also the coming of the Son of man be" (Mt.24:27).

QUESTIONS:
1. What kinds of fables do men design to try to save themselves? Do any of them work?
2. Do you believe in your heart that Jesus Christ actually came to earth to save you? How can you know for sure?
3. The world is full of evil and corruption. How does God intend to bring peace to earth?

2. THE FIRST PROOF OF SALVATION: THE GREAT EYEWITNESS ACCOUNT OF CHRIST'S MAJESTY AND TRANSFIGURATION (v.16-18).

The word "majesty" means the majesty of God, the *divine nature* of God.[2] It means that the *majesty and glory* of God filled and surrounded Christ when He walked upon earth. The early disciples and believers knew that Jesus Christ was the Savior of men because they saw the majesty and glory of God in His life and works. Jesus Christ went to great pains to reveal the majesty and glory of God; He proved time and again that He was the Son of God.

Now note verses 17-18: there was one event where the majesty and glory of God was allowed to shine out of Christ's very being; one event where the light of God's glory was so clearly seen that it proves beyond question that Jesus Christ is the Savior of the world, the very Son of God Himself. What was that event? It was the transfiguration of Christ. In the transfiguration of Christ, the very glory of God was *seen to be in Christ*. Scripture actually says that He was "transformed." The word transfiguration means a change into another form; to undergo a transformation, a change of countenance, a complete change. Luke said, "the fashion of His countenance was altered" (Lk.9:29). Note how the gospel writers described what happened.

"His face did shine as the sun and His raiment was white as the light" (Mt.17:2).
"His raiment became shining, exceeding white as snow; so as no fuller on earth can white them" (Mk.9:3).
"The fashion of His countenance was altered, and His raiment was white and glistening" (Lk.9:29).

---

[2] Michael Green. *The Second Epistle of Peter and The Epistle of Jude*. "The Tyndale New Testament Commentaries." (Grand Rapids, MI: Eerdmans Publishing Co., 1958), p.83.

Apparently *the glory* of His Godly nature was allowed to shine through His body to some degree. "The glory which [He] had with God before the world" shone through His body, shone right through His clothes (Jn.17:5). Peter said, "We were eyewitnesses of His majesty." In John's vision of Christ in <u>The Revelation</u>, he described the glory of Christ as "the sun [which] shineth in his strength" (Rev.1:16).

The scripture says:

"God is light" (1 Jn.1:5).

"[God]...<u>dwelling</u> in the light which no man can approach" (1 Tim.6:16).

"[God] who <u>coverest</u> thyself with light as with a garment" (Ps.104:2).

Peter, James, and John witnessed the event; they had the wonderful privilege of tasting a little of heaven's glory. They experienced the very presence of God Himself and tasted some of heaven's peace, joy, security, fulfillment, and perfection. Note that...

- they saw the honor and glory of Christ.
- they heard God call Jesus His Son; they actually heard God say, "This is my beloved Son, in whom I am well pleased."

Note also the exact words concerning the voice. The fact is repeated in both verse 17 and verse 18.

"There came such a voice to him [Christ]" (v.17).

"This voice which came from heaven" (v.18).

Peter emphatically stresses that they heard the voice from heaven. It was not a dream nor a vision nor a figment of their imagination. A voice from heaven actually called Jesus Christ His Son.

APPLICATION:

Peter unequivocally claims that he, the other apostles, and all the early believers witnessed the power and coming of the Lord Jesus Christ. He claims that they were eyewitnesses of God's great love, that God loves the world and has sent His Son into the world to save men. We either believe or do not believe their eyewitness account. It is that simple: we believe or do not believe their testimony.

"And the Word was made flesh, and dwelt among us, (and we beheld his glory, the glory as of the only begotten of the Father,) full of grace and truth" (Jn.1:14).

QUESTIONS:
1. If you were Peter, would you have believed that Jesus Christ was the Son of God? Why or why not?
2. Why is the transfiguration of Christ relevant to you today?
3. What caliber of witnesses were Peter, the other apostles, and all the early believers? How trustworthy are they? Are you trustworthy? Do you bear witness to Christ? To His saving power?

3. THE SECOND PROOF OF SALVATION: SCRIPTURE--THE MORE SURE ACCOUNT OF PROPHECY OR SCRIPTURE (v.19-21).

Note three significant points.
1. Scripture is more sure than an eyewitness account. There are an enormous number of prophecies in the Scripture about the coming Messiah and Savior of the world.

When they are studied, it is clearly seen that Jesus Christ is the promised Savior. He fulfills all the prophecies perfectly. Therefore, the prophetic Word is a much *more sure account* of salvation. Just by the sheer number of prophecies and their fulfillment in Christ, the Scriptures prove themselves to be a far greater witness to Jesus Christ. (See **A CLOSER LOOK, Prophecy--2 Pt.1:19-21** for a list of the Old Testament prophecies and their fulfillment in Christ.)

APPLICATION:

If the transfiguration of Christ had never taken place, the prophetic Scripture would still stand and prove that Jesus Christ is the Savior of the world. But if the prophetic Scriptures did not exist, the transfiguration by itself would be a much weaker proof that Christ is the Savior of the world. The transfiguration itself is greatly supported and substantiated by the prophetic Word. The prophetic Word helps tremendously to explain who Christ is and what was happening on the mount of transfiguration.

2.	Scripture is to be heeded. This is descriptive language: we are to heed the Word of God, for the Word of God is like "a light that shineth in a dark place, until the day dawn, and the day star arise in your hearts" (v.19). What does this mean?
⇒	The Word of God is like a light that shines in dark places. It shows us how to walk in the dark forest of this world. It reveals the narrow path to follow and exposes the stumbling stones and dangerous pits and poisonous creatures along the path.
⇒	The Word of God will show us how to walk "until the day dawn." What day? The glorious day of Christ's return. In that day, "the day star [Christ Himself shall] arise in our hearts" and perfect us. Our great salvation will be fulfilled and completed. We shall be transformed into His image, for we shall see Him as He is (1 Jn.3:2).

APPLICATION:

The point is this: we are to study and heed the Scripture. We are to study the Old Testament and the New Testament, the prophecies of Christ and the fulfillment of the prophecies by Christ. The Scripture is the light that guides us through this dark and dangerous world.

ILLUSTRATION:

It is one thing to memorize certain verses in the Bible. It is another to obey what you memorize. This is the story of a man who lived out what he memorized.

"There is a story of a missionary in Korea who had a visit from a native convert who lived a hundred miles away, and who walked four days to reach the mission station. The pilgrim recited proudly, without a single mistake, the whole of the Sermon on the Mount. The missionary was delighted, but he felt that he ought to warn the man that memorizing was not enough--that it was necessary to practice the words as well as to memorize them.

"The Korean's face lit up with happy smiles. 'That is the way I learned it,' he said. 'I tried to memorize it, but it wouldn't stick. So I hit upon this plan--I would memorize a verse and then find a heathen neighbor of mine and practice it on him. Then I found it would stick.'"[3]

Scripture is a sure proof of salvation, and it is the guideline for a believer's life. Are you just *reading* it or are you *heeding* it?

---

[3]	*Earnest Worker.* Walter B. Knight. *Knight's Master Book of 4,000 Illustrations,* p.26-27.

3. Scripture is not of any private interpretation (v.20-21). What does this mean? Verse 21 tells us. Men cannot interpret Scripture as they want. Scripture is to be interpreted by Scripture itself and by the Holy Spirit who dwells within the believer to teach him the truth. Note what verse 21 says.

    a. First, Scripture did not come from the will of man. No prophecy of Scripture arose out of the prophet's own interpretation. God moved upon the prophet's heart and gave him a vision and then the prophet wrote down exactly what the Spirit of God spoke to him. The prophet did not seek to place his own interpretation upon God's Word. Scripture is not of the will or mind of man. It is of God.

    b. Second, Scripture was given by the Holy Spirit. Men were moved (borne along, moved, impelled) by the Holy Spirit to speak the Word *from God.*[4]

> "For verily I say unto you, Till heaven and earth pass, one jot or one tittle shall in no wise pass from the law, till all be fulfilled" (Mt.5:18).

The point is this: Scripture can be trusted; it is the Word of God. Therefore, Jesus Christ is the Savior of the world. Man can be saved; his needs can be met. We can now have peace and life eternally. Salvation is now available through Jesus Christ our Lord. The proof is twofold: the eyewitnesses of the Lord and the prophetic Scriptures. Both prove beyond any question that Jesus Christ is the Son of God, the Savior and Lord of all men.

QUESTIONS:
1. Why is Scripture better than an eyewitness account? Has Scripture ever been wrong?
2. What dangers do you face if you fail to heed the Scriptures?
3. Why can Scripture be trusted? How much do you trust Scripture? Can you trust it even more? How?

A CLOSER LOOK:

(1:19-21) **Prophecy, Fulfilled--Scripture, Fulfilled**:

OLD TESTAMENT PROPHECIES OF JESUS AND THEIR FULFILLMENT IN THE NEW TESTAMENT

O.T. Reference	The Prophecy	N.T. Fulfillment
Gen.3:15	The Promised Seed of a Woman	Gal.4:4; Lk.2:7; Rev.12:5
Gen.12:3; 18:18; 22:18	The Promised Seed of Abraham	Acts 3:25; Gal.3:8 (Mt.1:1; Lk.3:34)
Gen.17:19; 22:16-17	The Promised Seed of Isaac	Mt.1:2; Lk.1:55, 72-74
Gen.28:14 (Num.24:17)	The Promised Seed of Jacob	Lk.3:34 (Mt.1:2)
Gen.49:10[a]	Will Spring From The Royal Tribe of Judah	Lk.3:33; Heb.7:14
Dt.18:15, 18	Will Be a Prophet	John 6:14; Acts 3:22-23

---

[4]   *From God* is the Greek phrase, A.T. Robertson. *Word Pictures In The New Testament*, Vol.6, p.159.

O.T. Reference	The Prophecy	N.T. Fulfillment
2 Sam.7:13[b] (2 Sam.7:13; Is.9:1, 7; 11:1-5)	Will be the Eternal Heir to David's Throne	Mt.1:1 (Mt.1:6; Lk.1:32-33)
2 Sam.7:14[a]	Will be God's Son	Mk.1:1
Is.35:6; 61:1-2 (cp.Ps.72:2; 146:8; Zech.11:11)	Will Meet the Desperate Needs of Men	Mt.11:4-6
Job 17:3	Will Ransom Men	Eph.1:7 (1 Jn.2:1-2)
Ps.2:1-2	Will Be Rejected By the Nations	Lk.23:36[a], 38
Ps.2:7	The Son of God	Acts 13:33; Heb.1:5; 5:5
Ps.8:2	Is to Be Praised	Mt.21:16
Ps.16:8-11	Will Be Resurrected	Acts 13:34-35; 2:25-28, 31 (Mt.28:1-2; Mk.16:6, 12, 14; Lk.24:1-53)
Ps.22:1	Will be Forsaken by God	Mt.27:46; Mk.15:34
Ps.22:7	People Will Wag Their Heads at the Cross	Mt.27:39
Ps.22:18	Clothes Gambled For	Mt.27:35; Mk.15:24; Lk.23:34; Jn.19:24
Ps.22:22	To Secure Many Brothers	Heb.2:12
Ps.31:5	Commends His Spirit to God	Lk.23:46
Ps.40:6-8	Fulfills God's Will	Heb.10:5-7
Ps.41:9	Is Betrayed by Judas	Jn.13:18; Acts 1:16
Ps.45:6, 7	Is Eternal & Preeminent	Heb.1:8, 9
Ps.68:18	Will Lead Captivity Captive	Eph.4:8-10
Ps.69:21	Offered Drugs on the Cross	Mt.27:48; Mk.15:36; Lk.23:36; Jn.19:28, 29
Ps.69:25; 109:8	Judas' Fate	Acts 1:20
Ps.89:26-27	Exaltation	Ph.2:9 (cp. Rev.11:15)
Ps.95:7-11	Hearts Hardened Against	Heb.3:7-11; 4:3, 5-7
Ps.102:25-27	Is Creator & Eternal	Heb.1:10-12
Ps.110:1	To Be Exalted	Mt.22:44; Mk.12:36; Lk.20:42; Acts 2:34, 35; Heb.1:13
Ps.110:4	The High Priest	Heb.5:6
Ps.118:22, 23	The Stone	Mt.21:42; Mk.12:10; Lk.20:17; Acts 4:11
Ps.118:25, 26	The Triumphal Entry	Mt.21:9; Mk.11:9; Jn.12:13
Ps.132:11, 17	The Son of David	Lk.1:69; Acts 2:30

O.T. Reference	The Prophecy	N.T. Fulfillment
Is.7:14	The Virgin Birth	Mt.1:23
Is.9:1, 2	A Light to Those in Darkness	Mt.4:15, 16
Is.11:2	The Spirit Rests Upon in a Special Way	Lk.4:18-21 (cp. Mt.12:18; Jn.3:34)
Is.11:10	To Save the Gentiles	Ro.15:12
Is.25:8	To Conquer Death	1 Cor.15:54
Is.28:16	The Stone	Ro.9:33; 1 Pt.2:6
Is.40:3-5	To Have a Forerunner	Mt.3:3; Mk.1:3; Lk.3:4-6
Is.42:1-4	To Minister to the Gentiles	Mt.12:17-21
Is.49:6	A Light to the Gentiles	Lk.2:32; Acts 13:47, 48; 26:23
Is.53:1	Would Not Be Believed	Jn.12:38; Ro.10:16
Is.53:3-6	To Die and Arise	Acts 26:22, 23
Is.53:4-6, 11	To Die for Man's Sins	1 Pt.2:24, 25
Is.53:4	To Heal & Bear Man's Sickness	Mt.8:17
Is.53:9	To Be Sinless	1 Pt.2:22
Is.53:12	To Be Counted a Sinner	Mk.15:28; Lk.22:37
Is.54:13	To Teach as God	Jn.6:45
Is.55:3	To Be Raised	Acts 13:34
Is.59:20, 21	To Save Israel	Ro.11:26, 27
Jer.31:31-34	To Make a New Covenant with Man	Heb.8:8-12; 10:16, 17
Hos.1:10-11	To Bring About the Restoration of Israel	Ro.11:1-36
Hos.1:10	The Conversion of the Gentiles	Ro.9:26
Hos.2:23	The Conversion of the Gentiles	Ro.9:25; 1 Pt.2:10
Joel 2:28-32	The Promise of the Spirit	Acts 2:16-21
Amos 9:11, 12	The Lord's Return & David's Kingdom Re-established	Acts 15:16, 17
Mic.5:2	The Birthplace of Messiah	Mt.2:5, 6; Jn.7:42
Hab.1:5	The Jews' Unbelief	Acts 13:40, 41
Hag.2:6	The Return of Christ	Heb.12:26
Zech.9:9	The Triumphal Entry	Mt.21:4, 5; Jn.12:14, 15
Zech.11:13	Judas' Betrayal	Mt.27:9, 10
Zech.12:10	The Spear Pierced in His Side	Jn.19:37
Zech.13:7	The Scattering of the Disciples at the Cross	Mt.26:31, 56; Mk.14:27, 50
Mal.3:1	The Forerunner, John the Baptist	Mt.11:10; Mk.1:2; Lk.7:27
Mal.4:5, 6	The Forerunner, John the Baptist	Mt.11:13, 14; 17:10-13; Mk.9:11-13; Lk.1:16, 17

1. How does this kind of study reinforce your faith?
2. In what way would you explain prophecies to an unbeliever?

A CLOSER LOOK:

(1:19) **"Word of prophecy"** is better translated *prophetic word*, referring to the whole prophetic message centered in Jesus Christ. The *prophetic word* did not begin or originate in the mind of man, but in the mind of God. However, God used men as instruments and authors to communicate His message to the world. Over a period of some 1500 years He chose kings, soldiers, peasants, farmers, scholars, priests, statesmen--approximately thirty-five authors from different nations, professions, and social strata. The original manuscripts were written in three different languages--Hebrew, Aramaic, and Greek.

1. The word *Bible* comes from the Greek word *biblos*, meaning *a book*. The Bible is also called "the Scriptures" (1 Cor.15:3-4) and "the Word of God" (Heb.4:12). The Bible is divided into two parts:
   ⇒ The first part, the *Old* Testament, was written before Christ.
   ⇒ The second part, the *New* Testament, was written after Christ came. The word *testament* means a *covenant or an agreement*. Therefore, the Bible is God's covenant, an agreement He has made with man. The Old Testament is His covenant with man before Christ came, and the New Testament is His covenant with man after Christ came.

2. The Old Testament has thirty-nine books which were designated as "the Law, the Prophets, and the Holy Writings or Psalms" (Lk.24:25-27). The books are sometimes divided as follows:
   ⇒ Five Law Books: Genesis, Exodus, Leviticus, Numbers and Deuteronomy. These five are known as the Pentateuch.
   ⇒ Twelve History Books: Joshua, Judges, Ruth, I and II Samuel, I and II Kings, I and II Chronicles, Ezra, Nehemiah, and Esther.
   ⇒ Five Poetic Books: Job, Psalms, Proverbs, Ecclesiastes, and the Song of Solomon.
   ⇒ Twelve Short or Minor Prophetic Books: Hosea, Joel, Amos, Obadiah, Jonah, Micah, Nahum, Habakkuk, Zephaniah, Haggai, Zechariah, and Malachi.
   ⇒ Five Long or Major Prophetic Books: Isaiah, Jeremiah, Lamentations, Ezekiel, and Daniel.

3. The New Testament has twenty-seven books which are sometimes divided as follows:
   ⇒ Four Gospels which cover the life of Christ: Matthew, Mark, Luke, and John.
   ⇒ One History Book which deals with the early believers and early church: Acts.
   ⇒ Fourteen Pauline Letters or Epistles written to specific churches or individual Christians: Romans, I and II Corinthians, Galatians, Ephesians, Philippians, Colossians, I and II Thessalonians, I and II Timothy, Titus, Philemon, and perhaps Hebrews.
   ⇒ Seven General Letters or Epistles written by other men to specific groups, each bearing the author's name: James, I and II Peter, I, II, and III John, Jude.
   ⇒ One Prophetic Book: Revelation.

4. The Bible has one central theme: Jesus Christ. He is the key to understanding what God reveals. He is the focal point of human history. In Him, God reveals His purpose and program for the ages (Heb.1:1-2).

5. The unity of the Bible is a miracle of God. Think of the facts: thirty-five different authors from unbelievably diverse backgrounds wrote over a 1500 year period. Think of the number and diversity of subjects, yet look at the harmony of purpose and theme. There is only one explanation. God has spoken and has preserved an authoritative record

message: "Holy men of God spoke as they were moved by the Holy Ghost" (2 Pt.1:21).

6.   The Bible claims to be the record of Jesus Christ (Jn.5:39), and it claims to be the written Word of God (2 Pt.1:21). As such, it is inseparably linked with the living Word of God, Jesus Christ (Heb.4:12; 1 Pt.1:23). Jesus Christ is the *living Word of God* and the Bible is the *written Word of God*. The written Word testifies to the living Word even as the living Word (Christ Himself) testified to the written Word.

QUESTIONS:
1. What kinds of writers did God use to record Holy Scripture? How does this authenticate the Bible as being the Word of God?
2. What is the central theme of the Bible? What would be the results if you took out the central theme of the Bible and replaced it with someone or something else? Has this happened in society?

SUMMARY:

God has supplied an abundance of trustworthy evidence, evidence that His salvation is authentic. You can know for sure, without a shred of doubt, that the salvation which comes through a personal relationship with Jesus Christ is real and lasting. The proof is in the Scriptures:

1.   The great truth: salvation is not a fable; it is the power and coming of Christ.
2.   The first proof of salvation: the great eyewitness account of Christ's majesty and transfiguration.
3.   The second proof of salvation: Scripture--the more sure account of prophecy or Scripture.

PERSONAL JOURNAL NOTES:
(Reflection & Response)

1. The most important thing that I learned from this lesson was:

2. The thing that I need to work on the most is:

3. I can apply this lesson to my life by:

4. Closing Prayer of Commitment: (put your commitment down on paper).

CHAPTER 2

II. THE WARNING AGAINST FALSE TEACHERS, 2:1-22

A. The Description & Judgment of False Teachers, 2:1-9

1. False teachers have always existed
2. False teachers teach destructive heresies

   a. The most tragic heresy: They deny the Lord
   b. The result: Swift destruction

3. False teachers mislead people
   a. They lead them to live in the flesh
   b. They cause slander
4. False teachers exploit people

5. False teachers shall be judged & destroyed

   a. God did not spare the angels who sinned

But there were false prophets also among the people, even as there shall be false teachers among you, who privily shall bring in damnable heresies, even denying the Lord that bought them, and bring upon themselves swift destruction.
2 And many shall follow their pernicious ways; by reason of whom the way of truth shall be evil spoken of.
3 And through covetousness shall they with feigned words make merchandise of you: whose judgment now of a long time lingereth not, and their damnation slumbereth not.
4 For if God spared not the angels that sinned, but cast them down to hell, and delivered them into chains of darkness, to be reserved unto judgment;
5 And spared not the old world, but saved Noah the eighth person, a preacher of righteousness, bringing in the flood upon the world of the ungodly;
6 And turning the cities of Sodom and Gomorrha into ashes condemned them with an overthrow, making them an example unto those that after should live ungodly;
7 And delivered just Lot, vexed with the filthy conversation of the wicked:
8 (For that righteous man dwelling among them, in seeing and hearing, vexed his righteous soul from day to day with their unlawful deeds;)
9 The Lord knoweth how to deliver the godly out of temptations, and to reserve the unjust unto the day of judgment to be punished.

b. God did not spare the old world, but He did deliver Noah

c. God destroyed Sodom & Gomorrah, but He did deliver Lot
   1) The cities were turned to ashes
   2) The cities are an example
   3) The reasons: Their immoral lives & the distress they caused for the souls of the righteous

d. God knows how to deliver the righteous & to reserve the unjust until judgment

Section II
THE WARNING AGAINST FALSE TEACHERS
2 Peter 2:1-22

Study 1: **THE DESCRIPTION AND JUDGMENT OF FALSE TEACHERS**

Text: **2 Peter 2:1-9**

Aim: To post a serious warning in your mind: Beware of false teachers!

Memory Verse:
> "The Lord knoweth how to deliver the godly out of temptations, and to reserve the unjust unto the day of judgment to be punished" (2 Peter 2:9).

INTRODUCTION:

If you were to take a wild guess, what percentage of the people in hell do you think got there because they were deceived? Probably the majority! What kinds of things deceive people into a false security: You name it: wealth, fame, religion, position, heritage, and on and on. At the root of all this deception is Satan. And how do you suppose he gets to people? One way is through false teachers--some within your own community, maybe even within your church.

If the world ever needed a warning, it needs to be warned against false teachers. Why? Because false teachers lead a person to doom himself quicker than any other single thing. Too many people are too quick to believe a lie. Why? So they can go ahead and live like they want. They want some excuse to get away from the restraints and demands that Jesus Christ puts upon them. Therefore, they grope after any teaching that lowers the Person of Christ. The more He is lowered, the less binding His demands are. But note: there is one major problem with false teaching. It is a lie; it is not the truth. A person dooms himself to an eternal hell if he follows false teaching. This is the critical message of this section of Second Peter: the warning against false teachers. This particular passage describes false teachers for us.

OUTLINE:
1. False teachers have always existed (v.1).
2. False teachers teach destructive heresies (v.1).
3. False teachers mislead people (v.2).
4. False teachers exploit people (v.3).
5. False teachers shall be judged and destroyed (v.3-9).

1. FALSE TEACHERS HAVE ALWAYS EXISTED (v.1).

They have always carried on their destructive work. Note the verse:

> "There were false prophets also among the people, even as there shall be false teachers among you" (v.1).

When did the false prophets do their destructive work in the world? When did the false prophets move among the people and introduce their destructive heresies? Note the previous verse along with this verse:

> "For the prophecy came not in old time by the will of man: but holy men of God spake as they were moved by the Holy Ghost. But there were false prophets also among the people, even as there shall be false teachers among you, who privily [secretly] shall bring in damnable heresies, even denying the Lord that bought them, and bring upon themselves swift destruction" (2 Pt.1:21-2:1).

The false prophets were at work while God was giving His Word to men. Imagine! Even while God was speaking and giving His Word to men, there were some who were denying His Word, teaching destructive heresies, and misleading people. There were false prophets all throughout the Old Testament period. They were the people who were denying God and His Word. But note: false teachers did not just exist in the Old Testament period. Scripture declares plainly: "there shall be false teachers among you." The idea is this: there will always be false teachers; false teachers will fill every generation of man and they will continue to introduce their destructive heresies until the world ends.

APPLICATION:

This means there are false teachers among us. We must, therefore, be alert to what every man and woman teaches. This does not mean that we should be on a witch hunt; it means that we should test all preaching and teaching by the Word of God.

> **"Beware of false prophets, which come to you in sheep's cloth-
> ing, but inwardly they are ravening wolves" (Mt.7:15).**

ILLUSTRATION:

How well do you listen when someone is teaching from the Bible? Each believer has a responsibility to discern what is being said. When you least expect it, a false teacher could be hard at work, sowing his seeds of corruption.

> *Years ago a young Christian man went to visit a church that had invited a semi-
> nary professor to speak at its revival. This professor received a great write-up in
> the church bulletin: "An earned Doctorate...Went to the finest schools...Has pas-
> tored many large churches...Has a marvelous voice."*
>
> *As this man preached, he said that sinners were not born; they were made. What
> he said was that original sin was a myth. "A person becomes a sinner only when he
> sins for the first time" he stated with a sense of intellectual pride.*
>
> *After the service was over, the young man approached the professor and said,
> "Sir, what about all the verses in the Bible that talk about original sin? How do you
> explain that away?" The professor looked at him sternly and said, "Young man,
> until you have all my degrees, don't you dare question my theology!"*
>
> *Walking out the door the young man said, "Professor, it is true I don't have your
> degrees, but I have something that your degrees could not give you--a love for the
> truth."*

How much do you love the truth? Enough to defend it?

QUESTIONS:

1. Where are false teachers most likely to be found? Why?
2. Is your church exempt from the possibility of false teachers? How can you guard against them?
3. Are you a good listener when others are teaching from the Bible? In what ways can you develop your listening skills?

2. FALSE TEACHERS TEACH DESTRUCTIVE HERESIES (v.1).

Note: Scripture says that false teachers secretly introduce or bring in destructive here-sies. They teach destructive heresies, but they do not do it openly. They do it deceptively, quietly, secretly, slipping in false doctrine here and there.

Note where false teachers teach their destructive heresies: in the church, right among believers. The false teachers are not out in the world, but they are within the church. They have joined the church and some have been outstanding members long enough to become teachers and preachers within the church. They hold leadership positions from which they can teach their destructive heresies. Note that the word "heresies" is plural. What are the heresies being referred to? Any teaching that goes contrary to the Scripture, that is, the Word of God or Bible. This is clearly what is meant, for the exhortation has just been given:

> **"Take heed to the word of prophecy, to the Scripture" (cp. 2 Pt.1:19-21).**
> **"[Scripture is the] more sure word of prophecy; whereunto ye do well that ye take heed...for the prophecy came not in old time by the will of man: but holy men of God spake as they were moved by the Holy Ghost" (2 Pt.1:19, 21).**

The point is this: any teaching that is contrary to God's Word is a destructive heresy. It destroys God's purpose for the church, and it destroys the lives of people within the church. Teachings that are contrary to God's Word are destructive and there is no escaping the fact. No matter how personable a person may be, no matter how much we may like him, if he is teaching a destructive heresy, he is destroying the church and the lives of people. William Barclay states it well:

> *"A heretic [is]...a man who believes what he wishes to believe instead of accepting the truth of God which he must believe.*
> *"What was happening in the case of Peter's people was that certain men, who claimed to be prophets, were insidiously persuading men to believe the things they wished to be true rather than the things which God has <u>revealed</u> as true. They did not set themselves up as opponents of Christianity. Far from it. Rather they set themselves up as the <u>finest fruits of Christian thinking</u>. Insidiously, unconsciously, imperceptibly, so gradually and so subtly that they did not even notice it, people were being lured away from God's truth to <u>men's private opinions</u>, for that is what heresy is."*[1]

1.   The most tragic heresy is the heresy that denies the Lord who bought us. Jesus Christ has bought us, and He has paid the supreme price to buy us. He gave all that He is and all that He has--even His life--in order to buy us out of sin and death. We owe our lives to Him; we owe everything to Him. The picture is that of a servant: we owe Christ our minds and hearts, our duty and service. Therefore, to deny Him is to deny our Lord and Master. And we all know what happens to the servant who denies his Lord and Master: swift destruction. No matter who the servant is, no matter how high a position he holds or how influential he is, if he denies his Master, he brings swift destruction upon himself. What does it mean to deny Christ? It means...

- to deny that Jesus Christ is the Son of God: that He left heaven above and came to earth as Man (the God-Man) to reveal God's great love for man.
- to deny that Jesus Christ is the Savior of the world: that He lived a perfect and sinless life and secured the perfect righteousness for man.
- to deny that Jesus Christ died *for man*: that He took man's sin upon Himself and bore the judgment and condemnation and punishment for man.
- to deny that Jesus Christ arose from the dead and conquered death for man.
- to deny that Jesus Christ is seated at the right hand of God to receive all the worship and glory and honor and praise of the universe.

The list could go on and on to include all that the Scriptures teach about Christ. To deny any teaching of Scripture about Christ is to deny Christ. This is the very point that Peter is making: we must take heed to the Scriptures...

- for the Scriptures have been given by God Himself (2 Pt.1:21), and there are false teachers among us.

---

[1]   William Barclay. *The Letters of James and Peter.* "Daily Study Bible Series" (Philadelphia, PA: Westminster Press), p.374. (Underlines are added by us for emphasis.)

APPLICATION:

Remember: these false teachers are in the church. They are the preachers and teachers who profess Christ and say that they are following Christ and building up His church. But what they are preaching and teaching is a complete denial of Him, and it is destroying the church. It could be compared to a drug dealer in a neighborhood school, someone no one would suspect. With his charm and false promises, he lures innocent babes into his web of addiction--only to doom them and himself to hopeless destruction.

> "Not every one that saith unto me, Lord, Lord, shall enter into
> the kingdom of heaven; but he that doeth the will of my Father
> which is in heaven" (Mt.7:21).

2.   False teachers shall be destroyed swiftly. Note that they bring destruction upon themselves. They are responsible for their own actions. They do not have to teach false doctrine; they make the choice to teach it. They could teach the truth [the Holy Scriptures], but they make a deliberate choice to teach contrary to what God has said. Therefore, they shall bring swift destruction upon themselves. The idea of swift is both certain and quick. When the judgment comes, there will be no discussion about the matter--no questioning, no leniency, no mercy, no love. There will be pure justice: swift, immediate judgment and destruction.

⇒   The word "destruction" means to lose one's well being; to be ruined; to be wasted; to perish; to be destroyed; to suffer perdition.

> "The Son of man shall send forth his angels, and they shall
> gather out of his kingdom all things that offend, and them which do
> iniquity; and shall cast them into a furnace of fire: there shall be
> wailing and gnashing of teeth" (Mt.13:41-42).

QUESTIONS:
1. False teachers are subtle in their deception. Why is this technique so effective?
2. Why are teachings contrary to God's Word so destructive?
3. What if a false teacher really believes what he is teaching? Is he excused? Why or why not?
4. Should false teachers be dealt with according to the seriousness of what they are teaching? Are some more dangerous than others?

3. FALSE TEACHERS MISLEAD PEOPLE (v.2).

False teachers do two terrible things.

1.   False teachers encourage people to live immoral and licentious lives. This is what is meant by *pernicious ways. Pernicious* means the ways of immorality and of the flesh. How do false teachers lead men to live worldly and fleshly lives?

a. False teachers say this: Christ is not the Son of God and the Bible is not the Word of God. But note this: if this is so, then there is no Lord over our lives and God has not told us how to live. There is no absolute authority over us, no absolute Word telling us how to live and how to get to God. The only authority that we have is the best thinking we as men can do. This teaching, of course, leads to worldly and fleshly living, for man cannot lead men above what he himself is. And man by nature is worldly and fleshly. If there is no absolute truth, no instructions telling us how to live, then we are free to live pretty much as we want just so we turn to some idea of God--some idea that we have of what He is like--

just so we turn to Him every now and then. And if God has not instructed us how to live--clearly instructed us--then He cannot hold us accountable if we mess up here and there. As stated, this kind of teaching lends itself to worldly and fleshly living. And remember: any religion and any philosophy that stresses that man is his own authority can go no higher than man. And man is worldly and fleshly by nature.

b. False teachers take the love of God and twist it. They say that God is so loving that He would never condemn man to an eternity of hell. They say a man must believe in Christ and follow Him, but if he fails, God still loves him and will forgive him and will never condemn and punish him--certainly not for long if at all.

Of course, the consequence of this teaching is devastating. For if a man thinks he is not to be judged and punished for his sin, he goes ahead and lives like he wants. He thinks he will never be condemned or punished for his sin, not for long if at all.

c. False teachers take the grace of God and faith and pervert them. They say that a person must believe in Jesus Christ. This, of course, is true: we are saved by believing in Jesus Christ; we are saved by grace through faith. But false teachers add that once we believe, we are okay forever and ever even if we do return to the world and live in sin. False teachers say that God accepts us even if we live like the devil and live after the world and flesh--just so we believe in Jesus Christ. False teachers say that faith exists without ever producing fruit: that a person can believe in Jesus Christ...

- without repenting
- without changing his life
- without separating from the world
- without denying and controlling his flesh
- without following Christ

False teachers say that God's love and grace are so inexhaustible that a man is free to sin just so he believes in Jesus Christ. The result of this teaching, of course, is the indulgence and license to sin. A man never has to worry about being rejected by God. He can live like he wants and sin as much as he wants just so he believes in Jesus Christ, for God's grace will forgive him and still make him acceptable.

"For they that are such serve not our Lord Jesus Christ,
but their own belly; and by good words and fair speeches deceive the hearts of the simple" (Ro.16:18).

2. False teachers cause the name of Christ to be abused. They cause people to speak evil of God, Christ, the church, believers, and the Scriptures. The very name of God is blasphemed because of hypocritical living and false profession. How often we hear comments such as "those hypocrites." Note that the blame lies at the feet of the false teachers. It is they who mislead people.

"Thou that makest thy boast of the law, through breaking the
law dishonourest thou God? For the name of God is blasphemed
among the Gentiles through you, as it is written" (Ro.2:23-24).

QUESTIONS:
1. If you live a loose, immoral life as a result of something you have been taught, you personally will pay the price. But how should false teachers be held accountable for misleading you?

2. Have you ever heard someone twist the love of God? Assuring you that God loves you, so much that He does not care if you sin or not? How does twisting the love of God affect people?
3. Those who cause people to speak evil of God, Christ, the church, believers, and the Scriptures are false teachers. What are some warning signs to look for.

4. FALSE TEACHERS EXPLOIT PEOPLE (v.3).

They use people just like they use merchandise: for their own ends. They are in the church ministering and teaching, but they are covetous, full of greed and lust. What is it that they are coveting?

⇒ popularity	⇒ attention
⇒ recognition	⇒ a following
⇒ a large church	⇒ success
⇒ livelihood	⇒ money
⇒ security	⇒ increased salaries
⇒ position	⇒ gifts
⇒ leadership	⇒ fame

A false teacher is often more interested in being popular and having the people accept him and his idea than he is in ministering to them. He is more concerned with a people following him, thinking he is a good teacher or preacher than he is in ministering to them. False ministers exploit people for their own ends.

> **"And he said unto them, Take heed, and beware of covetousness: for a man's life consisteth not in the abundance of the things which he possesseth" (Lk.12:15).**

ILLUSTRATION:

Can deception and exploitation happen in a normal church? Unfortunately, they can. Remember, the local church is sometimes the very place where a false teacher attempts to build his web.

> *Reg was a gifted teacher who had the ability to keep people on the edge of their seats. He was dynamic, interesting, and funny, which was a vast improvement over the classrooms where the lesson was read without conviction.*
>
> *Reg had an uncanny ability to get people to agree with him. But he could also be a pretty intimidating fellow, keeping people who wanted to ask questions in their place. By giving the impression that he was a great student of the Bible, no one felt comfortable challenging him on anything.*
>
> *One day he began to teach that serving in church was more important than the family, trying to build his own self-esteem and to win favor with the pastor. At first the people began to wonder, but "Reg must be right because he knows the Bible so well." Within a year, several of the marriages in that church had broken up because of what he had been teaching. Instead of working on the marriage--God's first ordained institution--these couples grew apart as they made it a point to be in church every time the doors were opened, oftentimes neglecting family.*

Do you care enough about your life to check out what your teacher is teaching? Remember: God's Word is the rule for your faith and practice--not the teacher.

1. What are some ways false teachers exploit people? Is there any justification for what they do? How can you stand up to someone who fits the description?
2. Some people treat the teacher as though he or she *knows all the answers*. Why is this so dangerous? Why is it so important to know what the Bible says?
3. Have you ever been exploited? Did you recognize it? What would you do differently if it happened today?

5. FALSE TEACHERS SHALL BE JUDGED AND DESTROYED (v.3-9).

Verse 3 is descriptive language. Upon earth it may seem that false teaching goes on and on forever without ever being corrected or handled by God. But no matter how successful or prosperous a false teacher may seem to be, judgment does not linger; it is not idle. The damnation of false teachers has not fallen asleep. The day is coming when all false teachers will pay for teaching destructive heresies. They will be damned, that is, destroyed, because they did not teach the truth of Christ and of God's Word.

Now, how do we know that false teachers will be judged and destroyed? Because God is God, which means that He is not only love but He is also *just*. He has the power not only to love people with a perfect love, but He also has the power to judge people with a perfect justice. Note four clear facts.

1. God did not spare the angels who sinned (v.4). He cast them down to hell. Eons ago in the distant past, Satan was apparently the highest created being ever created by God. At that time his name was Lucifer. But he did what so many people have done: he chose to go his own way; he rebelled against God. And he led a host of angels to rebel with him. Therefore, God judged him and cast him from his exalted position into hell. From what we can glean from Scripture, this is how Satan and the angels fell and became antagonists of God.

The point is this: even angels were cast down to hell and chained with darkness. And God is *reserving them for eternal judgment*. If God judged such glorious beings as Lucifer and the angels, how much more will He judge men, especially if they teach false doctrine and mislead people?

> **"By which also he went and preached unto the spirits in prison; which sometime were disobedient, when once the longsuffering of God waited in the days of Noah, while the ark was a preparing, wherein few, that is, eight souls were saved by water" (1 Pt.3:19-20).**

2. God did not spare the old world (v.5; cp. Gen.6:5f). The world had become totally wicked; wickedness prevailed in every mind, heart, and life.

> **"And God saw that the wickedness of man was great in the earth, and that every imagination of the thoughts of his heart was only evil continually" (Gen.6:5).**

He destroyed the whole world of the ungodly by a flood. God had no choice; His righteousness demanded that He judge the world of the ungodly. And this He did. God sent a flood of water to cover the world, and all the ungodly were destroyed. But note: there was one family saved--a preacher and his family. The preacher's name was Noah, and note what he preached: righteousness. He preached the righteousness of God. All the other preachers and priests of that day perished with all the other ungodly. But not Noah; he was saved, and the reason he was saved was because he was faithful to God and His righteousness. He lived and preached the truth of God and His Word.

The point is this: if God judged and destroyed the *whole world of the ungodly*, He will certainly judge and destroy a false teacher.

3.   God destroyed Sodom and Gomorrha (v.6-8; cp. Gen.19:1f). God caused an explosion, a combustion of fire to fall upon Sodom and Gomorrha. Note the facts of the outline:

a. The cities were turned into ashes (v.6).
b. The cities were made an example to all who live ungodly lives (v.6).
c. The reason for the judgment and destruction was twofold:
    ⇒ The citizens were living filthy, immoral, and unjust lives.
    ⇒ The sin and shame of the citizens were disturbing the heart of Lot. There was so much sin and shame that Lot's heart was distressed and tortured to see the law of God violated so much.

Note what happened: everyone in the city was judged and destroyed except one man, Lot. And note why he was saved--because he was righteous. (A study of Lot's life shows a selfish and carnal man; nevertheless, Lot believed God and when the time came, he separated from the ungodly and the world. He obeyed God.)

The point is this: if God judged and destroyed two great cities and all the people in them, he will certainly judge and destroy a false teacher.

4.   God knows how to deliver the godly and reserve the unjust until the day of judgment to be punished. This verse completes the sentence begun in verse 4. Note what it is that God delivers the godly from: temptations and trials; all the temptations and trials of life. There is no excuse for a false teacher preaching or teaching false doctrine--no excuse for him to fear other preachers or teachers or other men within his church nor to shy away from the truth--for God knows how to meet the needs of the man. God knows how to deliver the man from every obstacle and through every difficulty, no matter how great a trial or temptation. No matter who opposes the teacher, God knows how to deliver him. He delivered Noah and Lot both through the most trying opposition and ungodliness. But note this: God also knows how to keep the ungodly until the day of judgment and doom. All false teachers shall be judged and doomed to punishment.

"And fear not them which kill the body, but are not able to kill the soul: but rather fear him which is able to destroy both soul and body in hell" (Mt.10:28).

QUESTIONS:
1. What will be the destiny of the unrepentant false teacher? Is it harsh for you to warn him or her about God's judgment?
2. Does God have the right to judge a false teacher as harshly as He did the cities of Sodom and Gomorrah?
3. What promise does God make to the believer in verse 9? In what way is this a comfort to you?

SUMMARY:

Have you ever encountered a false teacher? As a believer, you have an obligation to protect yourself and your church from the sabotage of a false teacher. Important facts to remember are these:

1.   False teachers have always existed.
2.   False teachers teach destructive heresies.
3.   False teachers mislead people.
4.   False teachers exploit people.
5.   False teachers shall be judged and destroyed.

2 PETER 2:1-9

PERSONAL JOURNAL NOTES:
(Reflection & Response)

1. The most important thing that I learned from this lesson was:

2. The thing that I need to work on the most is:

3. I can apply this lesson to my life by:

4. Closing Prayer of Commitment: (put your commitment down on paper).

B. The Character & Conduct of False Teachers, 2:10-22

1. They walk after the flesh
2. They despise authority
3. They are presumptuous or arrogant
4. They are self-willed
5. They speak evil of dignitaries

6. They carouse around in pleasure & they do it openly, that is, along with the unbelievers of the world

7. They have eyes full of adultery
8. They entice unstable souls

9. They are covetous

10. They have forsaken the right way & gone astray

10 But chiefly them that walk after the flesh in the lust of uncleanness, and despise government. Presumptuous are they, selfwilled, they are not afraid to speak evil of dignities. 11 Whereas angels, which are greater in power and might, bring not railing accusation against them before the Lord. 12 But these, as natural brute beasts, made to be taken and destroyed, speak evil of the things that they understand not; and shall utterly perish in their own corruption; 13 And shall receive the reward of unrighteousness, as they that count it pleasure to riot in the day time. Spots they are and blemishes, sporting themselves with their own deceivings while they feast with you; 14 Having eyes full of adultery, and that cannot cease from sin; beguiling unstable souls: an heart they have exercised with covetous practices; cursed children: 15 Which have forsaken the right way, and are gone astray, following the way of Balaam the son of Bosor, who loved the wages of unrighteousness; 16 But was rebuked for his iniquity: the dumb ass speaking

with man's voice forbad the madness of the prophet. 17 These are wells without water, clouds that are carried with a tempest; to whom the mist of darkness is reserved for ever. 18 For when they speak great swelling words of vanity, they allure through the lusts of the flesh, through much wantonness, those that were clean escaped from them who live in error. 19 While they promise them liberty, they themselves are the servants of corruption: for of whom a man is overcome, of the same is he brought in bondage. 20 For if after they have escaped the pollutions of the world through the knowledge of the Lord and Saviour Jesus Christ, they are again entangled therein, and overcome, the latter end is worse with them than the beginning. 21 For it had been better for them not to have known the way of righteousness, than, after they have known it, to turn from the holy commandment delivered unto them. 22 But it is happened unto them according to the true proverb, The dog is turned to his own vomit again; and the sow that was washed to her wallowing in the mire.

11. They are filled with emptiness & instability

12. They speak great, pompous words of emptiness
13. They lure people through the lusts of the flesh

14. They promise liberty, but they only enslave people

15. The conclusion: A warning to false teachers
   a. Against returning to the world & its entanglements
      1) If one escapes the world's pollutions
      2) Then turns back
      3) The latter end is worse
   b. Against turning from the holy commandment

   c. Against becoming uncouth, repulsive to God

Section II
THE WARNING AGAINST FALSE TEACHERS
2 Peter 2:1-22

Study 2: **THE CHARACTER AND CONDUCT OF FALSE TEACHERS**

Text: **2 Peter 2:10-22**

Aim: To recognize the character and conduct of a false teacher: to avoid such conduct yourself.

Memory Verse:
> "For it had been better for them not to have known the way of righteousness, than, after they have known it, to turn from the holy commandment delivered unto them" (2 Peter 2:21).

INTRODUCTION:
One of the most frightening stories ever written was Mary Shelley's Frankenstein. You probably need no reminder, but this is the basic story: A dead man receives the brain of an insane man and then comes to life. Frankenstein, the monster, then terrorizes the community until he is destroyed.

A false teacher is just as threatening to the members of the local church. Whenever men take on the evil mind of Satan, a monster is created. Communities of faith are terrorized by present-day monsters who bring about lies and destruction. In the end, every false teacher will meet his doom and will be destroyed by God's judgment. In the meantime, how should the believer handle this monster?

This study is a graphic picture of false teachers. It shows how horrible God considers false teachers to be, and it serves as a severe warning to every person who would even dare to deny Christ and the teachings of God's Word. No matter who the teacher is--no matter how suave and charismatic, no matter how fluent and great an orator, no matter how creative and sharp a thinker, no matter how well liked and appreciated--if he teaches and denies Christ and God's Word, then he is a false teacher (cp. 2 Pt.2:1).

Here is one of the most horrible pictures painted in all the Bible. It is the picture of the character and conduct of false teachers.

OUTLINE:
1. They walk after the flesh (v.10).
2. They despise authority (v.10).
3. They are presumptuous or arrogant (v.10).
4. They are self-willed (v.10).
5. They speak evil of dignitaries (v.10-12).
6. They carouse around in pleasure and they do it openly, that is, along with the unbelievers of the world (v.13).
7. They have eyes full of adultery (v.14).
8. They entice unstable souls (v.14).
9. They are covetous (v.14).
10. They have forsaken the right way and gone astray (v.15-16).
11. They are filled with emptiness and instability (v.17).
12. They speak great pompous words of emptiness (v.18).
13. They lure people through the lusts of the flesh (v.18).
14. They promise liberty, but they only enslave people (v.19).
15. The conclusion: a warning to false teachers (v.20-22).

2 PETER 2:10-22

1. THEY WALK AFTER THE FLESH (v.10).

The flesh itself is not evil. It is what man does with the flesh that is evil. Man is both flesh and spirit. The spirit desires God; and the flesh desires food, security, recognition, love, companionship, and all the other necessities of life. But note: these are normal and natural desires. If we did not have these desires, we could not survive in the world. Again, man is both flesh and spirit. But note what the false teachers do: they walk after the flesh, in the lusts of the flesh. They ignore the spirit and follow the passions of the flesh. They indulge and gratify the flesh. They teach their false doctrine for personal gain. They desire...

- to live like they want.
- to gain recognition and honor and a following.
- to gain a livelihood and security.
- to gain worldly freedom and do away with godly restraints and demands.

As stated, the flesh desires these things and there is nothing wrong with them: a person needs recognition to feel that he is meaningful and significant. He also needs freedom and a livelihood. But when a person seeks more and more of these, when he takes the desires of the flesh and begins to lust after the desires, they become harmful and sinful.

⇒ One helping of food is good; two helpings are damaging to the body.
⇒ Some recognition is good; too much leads to pride and arrogance or indulgent selfishness.
⇒ Being free to secure the necessities of life is right, but trying to seek them without law leads to sinful transgression and lawlessness. As an example, we have all seen scenes of a community without law, all the looting and evil that runs rampant.

The point is this: false teachers walk after the flesh, not after the spirit. They are teaching in order to satisfy the flesh, to please people and to gain recognition, security, or livelihood. They teach a false doctrine in order to do away with the Lordship of Christ, for the Lordship of Christ demands the sacrifice of all one is and has. They want to live like they want, to do their own thing; therefore, they try to do away with the demands of God as much as they can. Again, false teachers walk after the flesh, not the spirit.

> **"For many walk, of whom I have told you often, and now tell you even weeping, that they are the enemies of the cross of Christ: whose end is destruction, whose God is their belly, and whose glory is in their shame, who mind earthly things" (Ph.3:18-19).**

QUESTIONS:
1. Why does a false teacher teach? What should be the correct motivation for teaching God's Word?
2. Is a false teacher submissive to God's leading? Why not?

2. THEY DESPISE AUTHORITY (v.10).

They stress rights, freedom, and liberty. They stress the right to live like they want, to do their own thing. They want few if any restraints or control over them. What is wrong with this? There is nothing wrong with rights, freedom, and liberty. But law is necessary, especially the law of God. Without God's law to control us, man becomes selfish and indulgent, and he gives license to his own personal desires. Without God's authority, man grabs for more and more; he takes more and more away from the earth and from the weaker people of the earth. This is a picture of the false teacher and his doctrine. He denies the Lord Jesus Christ. If Jesus Christ is not Lord, then His demand for self-denial and the sacrifice of all one is and has is not valid. The false teacher can pretty much live as he wants.

APPLICATION:

Despising authority within society is dangerous. What happens is that those in power create human laws that favor themselves, the rich and the powerful. Human law is not enough for man, for man cannot create a law higher than himself. Therefore, whoever is in power will always be influenced by some selfishness. He will seldom if ever give all he is and has to be perfectly just and equal to all. Therefore, God's law is necessary. Man must have a law that is above and beyond himself. Man must have a law that controls and governs all men. And more than this, man must have a living Lord who can give him the power and who can motivate him to live like he should. This is the reason the Lord Jesus Christ, who reveals and fulfills the law of God perfectly, must be proclaimed. He must be exalted and not denied. The only hope for man is to deny himself and give all he is and has to meet the desperate needs of *all the people and not of just a few.*

> **"Beware therefore, lest that come upon you, which is spoken of in the prophets; behold, ye despisers, and wonder, and perish: for I work a work in your days, a work which ye shall in no wise believe, though a man declare it unto you" (Acts 13:40-41).**

QUESTIONS:
1. False teachers despise authority. Why are they threatened by authority?
2. What is the true purpose of authority?
3. Why is it dangerous to despise authority within society? What would life be like without it?

3. THEY ARE PRESUMPTUOUS OR ARROGANT (v.10).

A daring spirit can be good; it can be courageous and brave. A person can set out on a daring venture for a good cause that reaps great benefits. But a daring spirit can be bad, very bad. A person can dare to do something that is difficult, but if it is wrong, he should not do it. His daring is nothing more than arrogance.

False teachers are daring and presumptuous. They venture into the theory of some false teaching, feeling courageous because they have the gumption to question God's Word and Christ. But note: this kind of daring is wrong. It is presumptuous. It is arrogance against the truth and against God.

> **"Be of the same mind one toward another. Mind not high things, but condescend to men of low estate. Be not wise in your own conceits" (Ro.12:16).**

QUESTIONS:
1. Can you think of an example when someone stepped over the line in questioning God's Word? Did he have the right?
2. In what ways is a false teacher arrogant against the truth and against God?
3. What kind of foundation has a false teacher built? Why are they doomed to failure?

4. THEY ARE SELF-WILLED (v.10).

They are set on doing what they want, and nothing is going to stop them. They are going to claim the right of free thought and free speech, the right to teach what they want. They are going to get what they are after, and no one is going to change them. The false teacher is going to share his opinion and denial of Christ and the Word of God even if it does hurt and damage others. Note the hardness of heart and obstinacy and stubbornness in this spirit.

"**For the heart of this people is waxed gross, and their ears are dull of hearing, and their eyes have they closed; lest they should see with their eyes, and hear with their ears, and understand with their heart, and should be converted, and I should heal them**" (Acts 28:27).

QUESTIONS:
1. What are some natural consequences of actions by a self-willed person?
2. Do you know anyone who is self-willed? What traits do they have that quench your spirit?
3. A false teacher is very opinionated. Do you ever struggle with a stubborn spirit? How can you overcome this?

5. THEY SPEAK EVIL OF DIGNITARIES (v.10-12).

This means speaking against, doubting, and questioning spiritual beings such as angels, cherubim, and seraphim. They ridicule the ideas of Christ and angels and other spiritual beings living in a spiritual world. They question whether there are even beings in a spiritual world, beings who are living and functioning just as we are in this world.
⇒ The idea of another dimension of being, of a spiritual world that is as real and alive as the physical world, is questioned.
⇒ The idea of levels of authority in a spiritual world or some other dimension, of principalities and powers and rulers in a spiritual world, is mocked.
⇒ The idea of Christ being exalted to the right hand of God, of believers someday ruling and serving and ministering for Christ in a new heavens and earth, is doubted and often ridiculed.

But note two things.
1. The angels themselves do not dare rail and mock the principalities and powers of the spiritual world. This is a strong warning to the false teachers.

"**For we wrestle not against flesh and blood, but against principalities, against powers, against the rulers of the darkness of this world, against spiritual wickedness in high places**" (Eph.6:12).

2. False teachers are like brute beasts who have no understanding. They are speaking of things they do not understand. No person knows what the spiritual world is like, for no person has ever been there. There is only one Person who has ever been there, and that is the Person who came to earth from the other world, the Lord Jesus Christ. He alone knows what the other world is like. This is the very reason He came to earth: to bring the Word and promise of heaven to us. We either believe Him or not. It is that simple. But note this: the Word of God is the prophecy and record concerning the Lord Jesus Christ. If a person does not believe Christ, then he has no right to claim to be a follower and minister of Christ. He should not abuse the Word of God through hypocrisy.

When he does he is as a brute beast, speaking of things he knows nothing about. And note what the Scripture says about him:

⇒ He is as a beast made to be taken and destroyed (v.12).
⇒ He shall utterly perish in his own corruption. That is, in trying to pollute the Word of God and Christ, he destroys lives; therefore, he shall be utterly destroyed. His own corruption shall destroy him.

> **"But if thine eye be evil, thy whole body shall be full of darkness. If therefore the light that is in thee be darkness, how great is that darkness!" (Mt.6:23).**

QUESTIONS:
1. Have you ever heard someone mock or ridicule the idea of angels? How did you respond? How should you respond?
2. Who has the right to speak about spiritual things? Have you ever spoken out of turn yourself about such matters?
3. What will be the outcome of the false teacher who abuses the Word of God?

6. THEY CAROUSE AROUND IN PLEASURE AND THEY DO IT OPENLY, THAT IS, ALONG WITH THE UNBELIEVERS OF THE WORLD (v.13).

They reject the Lordship of Jesus Christ and the strict demands of God's Word. Therefore, the demand for separation from the world and its pleasures and possessions are rejected. False teachers participate and share in the world, in its parties, social affairs, drinking, eating, smoking, and in being merry. They join in with the worldly, indulging the flesh. The ideas of Christian separation and sanctification are rejected by them. They reject the Lordship of Christ and His demand for total separation and self-denial and the sacrifice of all one is and has.

Note: Scripture says that false teachers are deceived. They think that sharing and participating in the world is acceptable. But they are wrong. They are spots and blemishes on the name of Christ and on the church. They soil and dirty the name *Christian*. They profess to be believers and are even teachers of God's Word, but they are not pure. Their worldliness--their partying, drinking, indulgence, and pleasure--dirties and blemishes the name of Christ.

APPLICATION:
Cults throughout the ages have been led by false teachers. Many of them are fanatical in their beliefs and practices--claiming to be followers of God, while at the same time participating in bizarre sexual games. They are deceived; they are following false teachers who are blemishing the name of Christ and Christianity. They are leading themselves and their cultists to destruction. There can be no compromise with the world and its ways.

> **"I beseech you therefore, brethren, by the mercies of God, that ye present your bodies a living sacrifice, holy, acceptable unto God, which is your reasonable service. And be not conformed to this world: but be ye transformed by the renewing of your mind, that ye may prove what is that good, and acceptable, and perfect, will of God" (Ro.12:1-2).**

1. Are you satisfied with your own separation from the world? What adjustments do you need to make in your lifestyle?
2. What explanations would a false teacher give about his choice to blend in with the world? Are any explanations acceptable?

7. THEY HAVE EYES FULL OF ADULTERY (v.14).

The world has always worshipped at the shrine of sex. Even today, in a society that has learned so much about human behavior and health, sex is used to sell everything from cars to soap. The human body is exposed to attract attention and to stir action whether to buy or to boost one's image. The result is loose morals and adultery.

The point is this: false teachers have chosen to deny Christ and the supreme authority of God's Word. Therefore, they feel more free to share in the ways of the world. By sharing in the worldliness of the world, they are attracted to look and think about the opposite sex. Thereby they are more easily aroused and stirred to desire. The result is catastrophic. They fall into immorality, desiring and lusting...

- to read or look at pornographic material
- to look at attractive bodies
- to make suggestive remarks
- to have adulterous affairs

But note: Christ is clear about the lust of the flesh and immorality.

> **"But I say unto you, That whosoever looketh on a woman to lust after her hath committed adultery with her already in his heart. And if thy right eye offend thee, pluck it out, and cast it from thee: for it is profitable for thee that one of thy members should perish, and not that thy whole body should be cast into hell. And if thy right hand offend thee, cut it off, and cast it from thee: for it is profitable for thee that one of thy members should perish, and not that thy whole body should be cast into hell" (Mt.5:28-30).**

1. In what ways can you protect yourself from the temptation of adultery
2. How can you make society a safer place sexually for your children, for the next generation?
3. Why is the promotion of sex so rampant in society? How has this effected the church?

8. THEY ENTICE UNSTABLE SOULS (v.14).

They trap people with their false teaching. They take people who are not grounded in the faith and lure them over to their opinion. They want the recognition or following...

- as a thinker or learned person
- as the creator of a new and creative idea
- as a great teacher or preacher
- as an influential leader

Whatever the reason, false teachers reach out with their opinions. They reach out to entice unstable souls to approve and accept their opinion.

"But woe unto you, scribes and Pharisees [religionists], hypo-crites! for ye shut up the kingdom of heaven against men: for ye nei-ther go in yourselves, neither suffer ye them that are entering to go in" (Mt.23:13).

ILLUSTRATION:

By definition, a false teacher's life is void of truth. In an attempt to be received by believers, false teachers will mask themselves with "spirituality." Author and pastor Warren Wiersbe illuminates this point with a personal story.

"In one of the churches I pastored, I noticed that a young man in the choir was doing his utmost to appear a 'spiritual giant' to the other choir members, especially the younger women. He prayed with fervency and often talked about his walk with the Lord. Some of the people were impressed by him, but I felt that something was wrong and that danger was in the air.

"Sure enough, he began to date one of the fine young ladies who happened to be a new believer. In spite of my warnings, she continued the friendship, which ended in her being seduced. I praise God that she was rescued and is now faithfully serv-ing God, but she could have avoided that terrible experience."[1]

The surest way to stay out of the wolf-trap is to stay in the sheep-fold--to be firmly grounded in the Word of God.

QUESTIONS:

1. Have you ever known someone who took advantage of a new Christian, an unstable soul? What influence did he have on the individual? How could it have been avoided?
2. Why does a false teacher tend to go after those who are not grounded in the faith?
3. How can your church protect itself from false teachers who prey on babes in Christ?

9. THEY ARE COVETOUS (v.14).

They are worldly minded, desiring the pleasures and possessions of the world...

• popularity	• success	• security
• attention	• money	• position
• recognition	• raises	• leadership
• a following	• gifts	• fame
• large churches	• livelihood	• possessions

They have coveted and coveted until their hearts are set on their worldly ambitions. They have continually struggled against God, conscience, Scripture, and what they know is right. They have focused upon their ambition and it alone, focused so much that their hearts are now trained to focus only upon their ambition. The truth of Christ and of God's Word no longer matter at all. All that matters is whatever the false teacher is after. Therefore, he persistently drives to get across his false doctrine.

Note: false teachers are said to be doomed, "accursed children." They are living under the curse of God and shall be destroyed.

"Thou shalt not covet thy neighbor's house, thou shalt not covet thy neighbor's wife, nor his manservant, nor his maidservant, nor his ox, nor his ass, nor any thing that is thy neighbor's" (Ex.20:17).

---

[1] Warren W. Wiersbe. *The Bible Exposition Commentary, Vol.2.* (Wheaton, IL: Victor Books, 1989), p.454.

1. Unfortunately, most people are worldly minded to some extent. But what is the difference in attitude between the average person and a false teacher when it comes to the pleasures of the world?
2. Can you identify anything worldly that has a hold on you? How can you overcome this enslavement?
3. Are you committed to focus your mind on Christ and heavenly things?

10. THEY HAVE FORSAKEN THE RIGHT WAY AND GONE ASTRAY (v.15-16).

Jesus Christ is the way to God. He said, **"I am the way, the truth, and the life"** **(Jn.14:6).** Therefore, if a person denies Jesus Christ, he has...
- forsaken the way to God
- forsaken the truth of God
- forsaken the life of God

The false teacher has forsaken the right way and has gone astray. He has forsaken the way that leads to life, following the way that leads to death. Note that Balaam is used as an example (cp. Num.22:1f). The king of Moab, Balak, began to fear the strength of Israel. Therefore, he sent messengers to a diviner named Balaam to come and put a curse upon Israel. At first Balaam refused to go and discuss the matter with the king. But the king continued to offer more and more position and wealth to Balaam. Finally the offer was so much that Balaam's heart coveted after the world. Therefore, he agreed to go and meet with the king. However, along the way, God gave the power of speech to the donkey that Balaam was riding and God rebuked Balaam through the donkey. Balaam was also the person who was later to turn Israel away from God and lead them into sin (Num.31:16; cp. Num.3:1f).

The point is this: Balaam is an example of a false teacher who became worldly and led God's people into sin and destruction. All false teachers who deny the Lord Jesus Christ...
- become worldly (seeking the possessions, acceptance, and security of the world) and forsake the right way and go astray.
- lead people into sin and destruction.

> **"Enter ye in at the strait gate: for wide is the gate, and broad is the way, that leadeth to destruction, and many there be which go in thereat" (Mt.7:13).**

1. Have you ever forsaken the right way and gone astray? Did you lead someone else astray in the process? How can you avoid doing this again? How do you keep from going your own way instead of God's?
2. How can you avoid being led astray by a false teacher?

11. THEY ARE FILLED WITH EMPTINESS AND INSTABILITY (v.17).

Two illustrations are given that describe false teachers.
- ⇒ They are like wells that offer water to travellers who have been crossing a dry, barren desert. But when the travellers reach the wells, they are dry.
- ⇒ They are like clouds that offer rain to the farmer. But when the clouds arrive, they are driven away by the rushing wind of a storm.

The picture is that of the false teacher offering hope to people, but his hope is empty and unstable, just as empty and unstable as the desert of the world itself. The false teacher cannot quench the thirst of people nor water the seed of God's Word in people's hearts. His false teaching is nothing more than the idea of a man; therefore, it ends up where all the ideas of men end--in the grave. The opinion of the false teacher cannot give hope at the end of life's journey nor in facing the trials and temptations of life. In dealing with eternity and God and Christ and Scripture, the false teacher is a well without water, as clouds driven away by the winds of a storm.

Note: the mist or gloom of darkness is forever reserved for false teachers. They are going to remain in darkness forever, both in this life and hereafter, unless they surrender to the Lordship of Jesus Christ.

> "This I say therefore, and testify in the Lord, that ye henceforth
> walk not as other Gentiles walk, in the vanity [emptiness] of their
> mind" (Eph.4:17).

QUESTIONS:
1. In your life, have you ever pursued something you wanted only to be sadly disappointed when you got it? This is what false teachers offer--false hope. How can you be sure of what you are being told and offered by a teacher?
2. A false teacher has more form than substance. Why is this true?
3. How long will the false teacher's darkness last? Is it worth whatever pleasure or possession he may gain while on earth?

12. THEY SPEAK GREAT POMPOUS WORDS OF EMPTINESS (v.18).

They use lofty words, excellency of speech, flowery language, and descriptive phrases; but what they say is empty. It is not the truth. It is only their own idea and opinion. As stated above, their false teaching can offer no hope, not in dealing with the trials and temptations of life and not in dealing with death. Their teaching ends up empty and unstable. Their teaching dies with the grave. It cannot carry us across the portals of death into life everlasting. Only Jesus Christ can do that. Therefore, if the teacher's message denies Jesus Christ, there is no hope of heaven, not a true hope.

> "The beginning of the words of his mouth is foolishness: and the
> end of his talk is mischievous madness" (Eccl.10:13).

QUESTIONS:
1. Why are so many people impressed with those who use flowery language?
2. Do you know someone who uses language like this? Does he impress you?
3. Is there a real benefit to the user of lofty words and excellent speech? What benefit?

13. THEY LURE PEOPLE THROUGH THE LUSTS OF THE FLESH (v.18).

Note who it is that the false teachers lure away: the immature believer and the young believer, those who have barely escaped the world. This is a warning to those who are not rooted and grounded in the Lord and in God's Word. Believers must be consistent in studying God's Word and in following Christ. This is the believer's only hope to escape the doom that is to fall upon those who follow false teachers.

14. THEY PROMISE LIBERTY, BUT THEY ONLY ENSLAVE PEOPLE (v.19).

Sin always enslaves. No matter what the false teaching is, it will enslave. The false teacher who denies Christ and God's Word removes the supreme authority over man's life. Therefore, man is pretty much free to live in selfishness and greed, desire and lust. He is pretty much left to seek as much pleasure and as many possessions as he desires upon earth. But in the end, man discovers something. The more he gets, the more he wants. It may be comfort, money, sex, position, or authority; it does not matter. Man's nature is such that he wants more and more. Man must be restrained by an authority above himself, that is, by God and by God's Word. If he is not, then he becomes enslaved to his passions and to the corruption of the world. This is one of the terrible fallacies of all false teachings. They all enslave man to this world: not a single false teaching can usher a man through the door of death into eternal life. Only Jesus Christ can do that. Note the clear truth: whatever overcomes a man, that very thing enslaves him.

⇒ If a false teacher overcomes a man, then the man is enslaved to that teaching.
⇒ If the world overcomes a man, then the man is enslaved by the world.

> "Jesus answered them, Verily, verily, I say unto you, Whosoever committeth sin is the servant of sin" (Jn.8:34).

15. THE CONCLUSION: A WARNING TO FALSE TEACHERS (v.20-22).

This is a strong warning to false teachers, a threefold warning.
1. Warning one: against returning to the world and its entanglements. If a false teacher once knew Christ and has returned to the world, his fate is going to be worse than if he had never begun with Christ. Why? Because he has known the truth and he has chosen to deliberately reject it. And even more, he is teaching against it. He has corrupted the truth of Christ and is leading others into destruction, dooming their very souls.

APPLICATION:
Teaching is the most responsible profession on earth. Therefore, the greater accountability falls upon the teacher's shoulders. God will have no mercy upon a false teacher; the false teacher will be judged much more severely than a person who never knew the truth.

2. Warning two: against turning from the way of righteousness and from the holy commandment.
⇒ The way of righteousness is Jesus Christ. He is the One who has made it possible for God to count us righteous and to accept us.
⇒ The holy commandment is the Word of God, that is, all the commandments of God.

It is far better for a person to have never known Christ or God's Word than to have known them and to turn back. The judgment shall be far worse, much more severe upon such persons.

3.   Warning three: against becoming uncouth, repulsive to God. The illustration given is clear. Imagine being compared to a dog that returns to its vomit and to a washed hog that returns to wallowing around in the foul, smelly mud. The judgment of God will be severe and terrible for all false teachers.

> **"And I saw the dead, small and great, stand before God; and the books were opened: and another book was opened, which is the book of life: and the dead were judged out of those things which were written in the books, according to their works" (Rev.20:12).**

ILLUSTRATION:
The false teacher will not escape God's judgment. The world is too small and God's memory is too great to allow him to miss his just reward. Here is a story of God's wrath upon a man who mocked Him.

> *"Seth Joshua, one of the leaders of the great Welsh revival of generations ago once arrived in a town where he was scheduled to preach and found placards everywhere announcing 'the Great Seth Joshua.' They told all about him but were in reality advertising a stage imitation of the minister at a local theatre that night. Grotesque drawings promised much fun at the expense of this servant of the Lord. That night the theatre was packed and the crowd cheered as the actor came on the stage in perfect imitation of preaching Joshua.*
>
> *"The actor raised his arms as he circled the stage burlesquing the Bible and the evangelist.*
>
> *"The third time around the actor fell with a thud and a hushed audience soon discovered that he was dead.*
>
> *"God will not hold [H]is wrath forever."*[2]

No one can mock God. No one.

QUESTIONS:
1. Do you ever wonder when God will judge false teachers? How does trusting God help you to allow Him to work in His time?
2. Are there false teachers whom you need to warn today? To pray for today?

SUMMARY:

A false teacher will leave a lasting impression on the fellowship of believers. It is time for the Christian believer to rise to the occasion and stand up to false teachers who have become monsters in the church. The first step is to recognize the character and conduct of the false teacher. In this study, we learned...

1.   They walk after the flesh.
2.   They despise authority.
3.   They are presumptuous or arrogant.
4.   They are self-willed.
5.   They speak evil of dignitaries.

---

[2]   Walter B. Knight. *Knight's Master Book of 4,000 Illustrations*, p.350.

6. They carouse around in pleasure and they do it openly, that is, along with the unbelievers of the world.
7. They have eyes full of adultery.
8. They entice unstable souls.
9. They are covetous.
10. They have forsaken the right way and gone astray.
11. They are filled with emptiness and instability.
12. They speak great pompous words of emptiness.
13. They lure people through the lusts of the flesh.
14. They promise liberty, but they only enslave people.
15. The conclusion: a warning to false teachers.

PERSONAL JOURNAL NOTES:
(Reflection & Response)

1. The most important thing that I learned from this lesson was:

2. The thing that I need to work on the most is:

3. I can apply this lesson to my life by:

4. Closing Prayer of Commitment: (put your commitment down on paper).

	CHAPTER 3	in the last days scof-	3. They walk after
		fers, walking after	passion
	III. THE SECOND	their own lusts.	
	COMING OF	4 And saying, Where	4. They scoff & ridicule
	CHRIST AND	is the promise of his	the return of Christ
	THE END OF	coming? for since the	
	THE WORLD,	fathers fell asleep, all	
	3:1-18	things continue as they	
		were from the begin-	
	A. The First Thing to	ning of the creation.	
	Know: Scoffers	5 For this they will-	5. They are willingly
	Shall Come, 3:1-7	ingly are ignorant of,	ignorant
		that by the word of	a. That God's Word
1. Arouse your pure	This second epistle,	God the heavens were	created the world
minds; arouse them	beloved, I now write	of old, and the earth	
so that you can re-	unto you; in both	standing out of the	
member	which I stir up your	water and in the water:	
	pure minds by way of	6 Whereby the world	b. That God's Word
	remembrance:	that then was, being	destroyed the world
a. Remember the	2 That ye may be	overflowed with wa-	
, words of the	mindful of the words	ter, perished:	
prophets	which were spoken	7 But the heavens and	c. That God's Word
b. Remember what	before by the holy	the earth, which are	reserves the world
has been preached	prophets, and of the	now, by the same	for destruction by
	commandment of us	word are kept in store,	fire
	the apostles of the	reserved unto fire	
	Lord and Saviour:	against the day of	
2. They come in the last	3 Knowing this first,	judgment and perdi-	
days, in our day & time	that there shall come	tion of ungodly men.	

Section III
THE SECOND COMING OF CHRIST
AND THE END OF THE WORLD
2 Peter 3:1-18

Study 1: **THE FIRST THING TO KNOW: SCOFFERS SHALL COME**

Text: 2 Peter 3:1-7

Aim: To stand prepared: Some persons will scoff at Christ's return.

Memory Verse:
> "Knowing this first, that there shall come in the last days scof-fers, walking after their own lusts" (2 Peter 3:3).

INTRODUCTION:
Do you recall the first time someone scoffed at your decision to follow Jesus Christ? The scoffing, the ridicule, hurt--probably cut deeply. Your feelings were hurt. After all, it was your commitment to follow the Savior of the world, the Lord Himself, that was being ridiculed. Did the scoffing discourage you? Discouragement comes in a variety of ways to the believer. One of Satan's most effective tools is the scoffer who ridicules Christians.

Have you ever had an argument with someone who was challenging your faith, but you forgot to say something that would have reinforced your point? "I wish I knew then what

I know now" or "I wish I had remembered to say 'this' or 'that'" is the testimony of many frustrated believers as they deal with scoffers. This study is designed to assist you in knowing what to say the next time you meet a scoffer.

The coming again of Jesus Christ and the end of the world--this is the subject of this final section of the book of Second Peter. This is a subject that literally fascinates tens of thousands of people. But note: fascination is not what God is after in discussing the return of His Son and the end of the world. What God is after is *preparation*--for man to prepare himself to receive God's Son. Man must be ready for the return of Christ or else he will be doomed. This first passage covers a critical subject: *The first thing to know--scoffers shall come*.

OUTLINE:

1. Arouse your pure minds; arouse them so that you can remember (v.1-2).
2. They come in the last days, in our day and time (v.3).
3. They walk after passion (v.3).
4. They scoff and ridicule the return of Christ (v.4).
5. They are willingly ignorant (v.5-7).

1. AROUSE YOUR PURE MINDS; AROUSE THEM SO THAT YOU CAN RE-MEMBER (v.1-2).

If a person is to know and understand the return of the Lord, his mind has to be aroused. The mind cannot be lazy or wandering about. It has to be watchful, alert, focused, concentrated, and actively engaged upon two things.

First, the mind must remember the words spoken by the prophets. They had much to say about the return of Christ to earth.

Second, the mind must remember the commandments of the Lord that have been preached and taught by the apostles. Jesus Christ taught much about His return. The apostles in turn shared His teachings with their people.

The importance of the mind being aroused cannot be over-stressed. Note how Peter drives the point home:

⇒ "Stir up your pure minds" (v.1)
⇒ "Be mindful" (v.2)
⇒ "Know this first" (v.3)
⇒ "Do not be ignorant of this one thing" (v.8)

The phrase "pure minds" means to have a clear, pure, unmixed, uncontaminated, focused, and concentrated mind. It is the picture of thoughts being sifted just like wheat is sifted in order to be separated from the chaff. Thoughts are to be sifted in order to separate the true and pure from the untrue and impure. There is always so much false teaching about the end time that the mind must be pure in order to sift the true teaching from the false. The picture of a pure mind is this: the mind must be exposed to the light of the sun and be found flawless. The mind must be pure and clear from wandering and impure thoughts if it is to study the Word of God and learn its great teachings. The mind must be pure and clear if it is to grasp the great truth of the return of Jesus Christ to earth.

Note one other fact in these first two verses: the unity of Scripture. The prophets of the Old Testament, the words of Jesus Christ, and the preaching and teaching of the apostles are all tied together and put on an equal footing--at least by the time the letter of Second Peter was written. They were all considered to be authoritative, to be the Word of God. Note that Paul's writings were also considered to be Scripture by Peter when he was writing this letter (v.15-16). Paul's writings were already considered to be the very Word of God to men.

APPLICATION:

The stress is upon the mind--a pure and clear mind, a mind that is focused and learning and remembering what it has been taught. But note this: before a person can remember something, he first has to study and learn the facts. This stresses the utter necessity for him to study the Scriptures, to learn all he can about the return of Christ to earth. There is no place in the Christian life for lazy, lethargic, unfocused, and wandering minds. Christ demands total dedication from a person, the total commitment of a person's mind and life to His teaching. This requires intense and diligent study of the Word of God.

This also speaks directly to preachers and teachers. The early apostles studied the prophets and the words of Jesus. They studied the Scripture; therefore they knew all about the return of Christ to earth. Consequently, they were able to offer great hope to their people, the great hope of the second coming of Christ to earth.

QUESTIONS:

1. In practical terms, what does it mean to have a pure mind? What one thing can you do today to keep your mind pure?
2. What is your mind supposed to be focused on the most? Has this been a regular habit in your life? Why or why not?
3. Having an on-going study time in God's Word is so important for the believer. How disciplined are you in Bible study? How can you improve this area of your life?

2. THEY COME IN THE LAST DAYS, IN OUR DAY AND TIME (v.3).

The first coming of Jesus Christ to earth was the pivotal point of human history.
⇒ Jesus Christ came in "the fulness of time" (Gal.4:4).
⇒ Jesus Christ came "in these last times for you" (1 Pt.1:20).
⇒ God has "in these last days spoken unto us by His Son" (Heb.1:2).
⇒ John the Apostle says, "it is the last time" (1 Jn.2:18).

Since Jesus Christ first came to earth, history is in its last stage. Right now, the time between Christ's first coming and His second coming, is called the age of grace--the age when God's mercy and grace are flowing out to the world through His Son, the Lord Jesus Christ. The thing to remember is that this period of history is called...
• "these last times" (1 Pt.1:20).
• "the last days" (2 Pt.3:3; 2 Tim.3:1).
• "these last days" (Heb.1:2).
• "the last time" (1 Jn.2:18; Jude 18).

Note John's term for the end time: "the last time." The Greek really means the last hour, the midnight hour when the world is to end. But note this: the end time does not mean annihilation; it does not mean that everything will cease to exist. As William Barclay describes so well:

> "In biblical thought the last time is the end of one age and the beginning of another. It is not only a time of ending; it is a time of new beginning. It is not only a time of destruction; it is a time of re-creation. It is last in the sense that things as they are pass away; but leads not to world obliteration, but world re-creation. In other words, the last hour and the last days lead not to extinction, but to consummation."[1]

---

[1] William Barclay. *The Letters of John and Jude.* "The Daily Study Bible," p.71.

The final chapter of human history is now being written. Soon Jesus Christ will return to earth and time will be no more. When? Jesus Christ said that no man knows nor can know. Only God knows. And we must always keep in mind what verse eight says, "that a thousand years is as one day" with the Lord. Therefore, we must not be projecting dates. What we must do is obey the Lord's exhortation to watch and be ready. We are to look for His return every day and be prepared for His return any moment. And when He returns, not only will the earth and the heavens be destroyed, but He is going to re-create the whole universe, both the heavens and the earth. The new universe will be the home of all those who have followed Jesus Christ.

APPLICATION:

This then is the message that we must heed: it is the *last days*. What are we going to do about it? Are we going to attach ourselves to the world and be destroyed with it or attach ourselves to Jesus Christ and enter into the glory of the new world that is soon coming? The choice is ours. We either follow the world that is doomed to destruction or else we follow Jesus Christ and enter the new world promised by Him. The end time, the destruction of the world that is coming, is not a message of gloom; it is the most glorious message of hope--the hope of a new world. There is a new world coming that will be gloriously perfected: no corruption, evil, sin, or death--only glory and splendor, health and life; and it will last forever and ever, world without end.

But note the point: there are scoffers in these last days, people who scoff at the idea of Christ returning to earth and re-creating the universe. Three significant facts are said about the scoffers. The next three main outline points discuss these facts.

> "Then certain philosophers of the Epicureans, and of the Stoics, encountered him. And some said, What will this babbler say? other some, He seemeth to be a setter forth of strange gods: because he preached unto them Jesus, and the resurrection" (Acts 17:18).

QUESTIONS:
1. Do you believe you are living in the last days? If so, what is to be your attitude toward life? If not, can you afford to take a chance and live like you want? What if you are wrong?
2. Considering the gloomy outlook for unbelievers, are you doing your part to share the gospel with them?

3. THEY WALK AFTER PASSION (v.3).

They live like they want and do their own thing. They want the possessions and pleasures of this world.
⇒ They want the right to seek and keep as much as they can of money, houses, lands, furnishings, recognition, popularity, honor, position, authority, power, fame, recreation, comfort.
⇒ They want the right to enjoy all the pleasure they feel safe doing such as partying, drinking, eating, and engaging in suggestive immoralities and sexual relationships.

These are the mockers, people who walk after their own lusts. They have to mock and reject the second coming of Christ. If they accepted it, they would have to change their lives; they would have to repent and turn to Christ or else live under the terrible fear of eternal judgment. They are unwilling to change their lives; therefore, they reject Jesus Christ and His return to earth in judgment.

"Now the works of the flesh are manifest, which are these; Adultery, fornication, uncleanness, lasciviousness, idolatry, witchcraft, hatred, variance, emulations, wrath, strife, seditions, heresies, envyings, murders, drunkenness, revellings, and such like: of the which I tell you before, as I have also told you in time past, that they which do such things shall not inherit the kingdom of God" (Gal.5:19-21).

ILLUSTRATION:
The scoffer makes it a habit to live on the brink of disaster. The life of a modern-day scoffer life can be compared to this story.

"As part of a circus act, a man would place his head in a tiger's mouth! He advanced to the tiger and the tiger opened his mouth. While the crowd watched in breathless wonder and horror, the man thrust his head in the open mouth, paused a moment, then slowly withdrew his head from the place of danger and backed from the cage. As he shut the door, the tiger leaped against the bars with terrific force.

"Such a foolhardy stunt was sure to attract much attention, and many prophesied that some day that man would pay for his foolishness. Their utterance was filled. In a small town in northern Pennsylvania the man met his doom. While his head was in the tiger's mouth, those powerful jaws closed on him, and before several bullets ended the tiger's life, the man was a corpse.

"This takes us in thought to two verses in the Epistle of James: 'But every man is tempted, when he is drawn away of his own lust, and enticed. Then when lust hath conceived, it bringeth for sin; and sin, when it is finished, bringeth forth death.'"[2]

Lust can turn anyone's head and blind him to danger. Is your head on straight or is it in the mouth of the tiger?

QUESTIONS:
1. How can you keep yourself from being consumed by lust?
2. Why is a scoffer comfortable walking after his own lusts? In what way is this a warning to you?
3. What will be the destiny of a scoffer who walks after his own lusts? Will it be worth what he might have possessed on this earth?

4. THEY SCOFF AND RIDICULE THE RETURN OF CHRIST (v.4).

They scoff for two reasons.
1.   They scoff because it has been thousands of years since Jesus Christ came to earth the first time. They scoffingly ask:
"Where is the promise of Christ's return? What has happened to His promise? It has been thousands of years since He first came, and Christians have always been proclaiming that He was coming soon. Even today you are declaring that He is coming soon, declaring that His coming is just around the corner, declaring that everyone must expect His return today. What has happened? Where is He? If He was coming back to earth, He would have surely returned by now."

---

[2] *L.L. Wightman, in Gospel Herald.* Walter B. Knight. *Knight's Master Book of 4,000 Illustrations,* p.626.

Some mockers even argue this: "There is so much suffering and evil in the world, Christ would certainly have returned by now if He was going to. He would have returned and brought the peace and abundance of life that Christians proclaim."

Note: the first argument of the scoffers is based upon the teaching that the second coming is false. They feel that Christ would have returned long ago if the teaching were true. The fact that He has not yet returned proves that the teaching of the second coming is false. Christ is not returning to earth. A person can, therefore, forget the doctrine and go ahead and live as he wishes.

> "For as the lightning cometh out of the east, and shineth even unto the west; so shall also the coming of the Son of man be....But of that day and hour knoweth no man, no, not the angels of heaven, but my Father only" (Mt.24:27, 36).

2.   They scoff because the world continues on just as it always has. They argue: "There has never been a change in the way the world operates; there has not been a change since creation itself, not a convulsive event that would shake the world like the return of Jesus Christ to earth in a world-wide judgment."

Note: this second argument is based upon the stability of the universe and its laws, upon the fact that the laws of nature run the world and keep it stable and functioning. The laws of nature have kept the universe running on and on without any major convulsive event. Therefore they argue:

"Why then should people get excited and become concerned about the world ending? The laws of nature run the universe, not an imaginary God. Nothing has ever changed the world; the world has been going on for millions of years. In fact, it has been continuing on for thousands of years since Christ came. Why then get concerned about a change now? The laws of nature will continue to run the universe and keep it stable."

> "And I will say to my soul, Soul, thou hast much goods laid up for many years; take thine ease, eat, drink, and be merry" (Lk.12:19).

QUESTIONS:
1. Why do scoffers ridicule the return of Christ? Have you ever wondered or questioned about the very reasoning the scoffers use, whether they might be right? How can you know the truth?
2. How can you refute the arguments of the scoffers?

5. THEY ARE WILLINGLY IGNORANT (v.5-7).

The scoffers are ignorant of three facts, and note, Scripture says that they are *willingly ignorant*. They choose to ignore, to be unreasonable, and to reject the fact that God is the Creator and Sustainer of the world. Note these facts.

1.   Scripture declares that the world is not self-creating and self-sufficient (v.5). It was not made by the laws of nature and it does not run and operate itself by the laws of nature. The heavens and earth were created by *the Word of God*. It was God, His speaking the world into existence, who created the universe and the laws of nature. The heavens and earth were created by God simply speaking and bringing them into being. God is God, the Supreme Intelligence and Power; therefore, God can simply will and speak, and His Word creates whatever He wills.

The point is this: mockers willingly choose to ignore and reject God, to deny God's absolute intelligence and power. Therefore, they are willingly ignorant that God created the world and that He sustains it by the mere power of His Word. The world and its laws are existing today only because God keeps them existing today. The only reason Jesus Christ has not yet returned to earth is because it is not yet God's time. God is not yet ready for Christ to return. When God's day arrives, God will simply speak the Word and Christ will return. The final chapter of human history will then be closed.

> **"Through faith we understand that the worlds were framed by the word of God, so that things which are seen were not made of things which do appear" (Heb.11:3).**

2. Scripture declares that the world has not always continued on as it presently does (v.6). The idea that world-wide convulsive events do not happen is totally false. The earth has perished before; God spoke the Word and judged the world. His Word destroyed the world with a flood and all life was destroyed except Noah and his family and two of every creature. God did not let people go on and on in their sin forever. God judged and punished sinners. The world is a moral universe. God created it to be moral, and He expects man to live righteous and godly lives while here on earth. If they refuse, then He speaks His Word and judges the earth.

Again, note that the mockers willingly choose to ignore and reject the facts about a flood that destroyed all of life. The bones and the imprint of the bones of sea life can be found all over the dry land of the earth, yet men continue to reject the evidence of a cataclysmic flood that destroyed life upon earth. They ignore and reject that this is a moral universe that is answerable to a loving and just God. They reject Him because they want to control their own lives and live as they wish (v.3).

The point is this: the world was destroyed by God's Word once; it can, therefore, be destroyed by God's Word again. One cataclysmic destruction took place; therefore, another catastrophic destruction can occur. In fact, the only reason the world has not yet been destroyed is that it is not yet God's time. But Scripture is clear; God has spoken: Jesus Christ is going to return to the world and the world is going to be judged and destroyed again.

> **"But of that day and hour knoweth no man, no, not the angels of heaven, but my Father only. But as the days of Noe were, so shall also the coming of the Son of man be. For as in the days that were before the flood they were eating and drinking, marrying and giving in marriage, until the day that Noe entered into the ark, and knew not until the flood came, and took them all away; so shall also the coming of the Son of man be" (Mt.24:36-39).**

3. Scripture declares that the heavens and earth are being kept, reserved, and stored up for destruction by fire (v.7). How? By God's Word. God is controlling the heavens and the earth. They have not yet been destroyed because God has not yet spoken the Word. But note: he is keeping, reserving, and storing up the world for destruction by fire. Why? Because of ungodly men. As stated, this is a moral universe and God expects men to live moral and pure lives. The day of judgment and perdition (destruction) is coming because men have chosen to live ungodly lives. It is this that men and mockers have chosen to ignore and reject: they are accountable to a loving, holy, and just God. It is this that they refuse to study and know and submit to. Therefore, they continue on in their selfish, hoarding, unjust, and immoral ways. And they continue to scoff at the coming again of the Lord Jesus Christ to judge the earth.

> **"When the Son of man shall come in his glory, and all the holy angels with him, then shall he sit upon the throne of his glory: and before him shall be gathered all nations: and he shall separate them**

one from another, as a shepherd divideth his sheep from the goats"
(Mt.25:31-32).

ILLUSTRATION:

Scoffers are *willingly ignorant*. In other words, like an ostrich, they have chosen
to hide their heads in the sands of denial.

> *Legend has it that the ostrich overheard Chicken Little say the sky was fal-
> ling. Fearing for his life, the ostrich hid his head in the sand. Thinking to him-
> self, the ostrich said, "I'll be safe if I do not see anything bad."*
> *And so, the ostrich kept his head in the sand. One of his animal friends
> walked by and said, "Ostrich, why is your head in the sand?" With a voice muf-
> fled by the sand, the ostrich said, "Chicken Little said the sky is falling. If I
> can't see it I'll be safe."*
> *"But Ostrich" said the animal friend, "I think Chicken Little is wrong. The
> sky is not falling. Why don't you look up for yourself and see?" And the friend
> walked on.*
> *Another animal came upon the ostrich who still had his head hidden in the
> sand. "Ostrich, why is your head buried in the sand?" said the animal. Again,
> with a muffled voice, "Because if I can't see the end of the world, I won't get
> hurt." "Great idea" said the lion. Then he took a vicious bite and had the os-
> trich for his dinner.*

The scoffer is a lot like this ostrich. Denying that he is in eternal danger does
not change a thing. One day the Lamb of God will have a great banquet. Will you
be His invited guest or will you end up as a part of the menu of judgment?

QUESTIONS:

1. Do you know someone who is "willingly ignorant" about Christ's return? What
   is his reasoning, his motive?
2. Why does a scoffer have such a difficult time confessing God's creation of the
   heavens and earth? Is it true ignorance? Rebellion against God? Exaltation of
   man? A desire to live like he wants, free from the righteousness demanded by
   God?
3. What comfort can you take in the knowledge that God *will* destroy the world? In
   the fact that God *has withheld* His destruction of the world until now?

SUMMARY:

Scoffers not only *will* come in the future, they are already *here*. It is up to you to be
able to recognize someone who scoffs at Christ's return--and then be able to respond. The
first thing that you need to remember is:

1.   Arouse your pure mind; arouse it so you can remember.

Then remember that scoffers...

2.   Will come in the last days, in our day and time.
3.   Walk after passion.
4.   Scoff and ridicule the return of Christ.
5.   Are willingly ignorant.

2 PETER 3:1-7

PERSONAL JOURNAL NOTES:
(Reflection & Response)

1. The most important thing that I learned from this lesson was:

2. The thing that I need to work on the most is:

3. I can apply this lesson to my life by:

4. Closing Prayer of Commitment: (put your commitment down on paper).

	B. The One Thing Not to be Ignorant About: Why Christ Has Not Yet Returned, 3:8-10	count slackness; but is long-suffering to us-ward, not willing that any should perish, but that all should come to repentance.	longsuffering, cp. v.15 a. He wants none to perish b. He wants all to repent
1. The Lord does not measure time the same as man	8 But, beloved, be not ignorant of this one thing, that one day is with the Lord as a thousand years, and a thousand years as one day.	10 But the day of the Lord will come as a thief in the night; in the which the heavens shall pass away with a great noise, and the elements shall melt with fervent heat, the	3. The Day of the Lord is coming a. As a thief—unexpected b. The heavens will pass away with a great noise c. The elements will melt with intense heat
2. The Lord is not slow in sending Christ back to earth, but is	9 The Lord is not slack concerning his promise, as some men	earth also and the works that are therein shall be burned up.	d. The earth will burn up e. All things shall be dissolved

Section III
THE COMING AGAIN OF CHRIST
AND THE END OF THE WORLD
2 Peter 3:1-1

Study 2: **THE ONE THING NOT TO BE IGNORANT ABOUT: WHY CHRIST HAS NOT YET RETURNED**

Text: **2 Peter 3:8-10**

Aim: To trust God's timing: Christ will return *in God's time.*

Memory Verse:
> "The Lord is not slack concerning his promise, as some men count slackness; but is long-suffering to us-ward, not willing that any should perish, but that all should come to repentance" (2 Peter 3:9).

INTRODUCTION:

Everyone has probably played "hide-and-seek" in his life. The rules of this game are pretty simple. One player hides his eyes and counts to 100 (or some other agreed upon number) while the other player runs off to hide. When the count is over, the player who counted cries out, "Ready or not. Here I come!" Then he or she scampers off to find the one who is hiding. If the person who is hiding has done a really good job and cannot be found, the person searching calls out in surrender and says, "I give up!" and the person who has been hiding races home.

Have you ever felt as though Jesus Christ were hiding? As though He were far, far away--out of reach? As you see the state of the world, you might have even cried out to Him "I give up!" in hopes that your cry would hasten the return of Christ.

Jesus Christ is coming back to earth. This is the declaration of Scripture time and again.

> "Jesus saith unto him, Thou hast said: nevertheless I say unto you, Hereafter shall ye see the Son of man sitting on the right hand of power, and coming in the clouds of heaven" (Mt.26:64).

Every generation of believers has proclaimed that Jesus Christ is *coming soon*. Even believers today proclaim that He is returning and that His return is just over the horizon. But it has been two thousand years since these promises were made. Does this mean then that the teaching of His return is false, that Jesus Christ is not going to return to earth? Have Christians been wrong in declaring that Jesus Christ was to return soon? How can thousands of years be said to be soon? There are those who ask questions like this and there are even those who use these questions to mock the return of Christ. The mockers of the second coming of Christ were the discussion of the former passage (see outline-- 2 Pt.3:1-7 for discussion). But what are the answers to these questions? Why has Christ not yet returned? This is the one thing we must not be ignorant about: *Why Christ has not yet returned to earth.*

OUTLINE:
1. The Lord does not measure time the same as man (v.8).
2. The Lord is not slow in sending Christ back to earth, but is longsuffering (v.9).
3. The Day of the Lord is coming (v.10).

1. THE LORD DOES NOT MEASURE TIME THE SAME AS MAN (v.8).

Why has Christ not yet returned to earth? First, because God does not measure time the same as man. There are two differences between the time of God and the time of man.

1. There is the *span of time*. To God, a thousand years is *only as one day*. God is eternal. Think of thousands of years heaped upon thousands of years. Multiply ten thousand years times ten thousand and then multiply that by thousands of years again and keep on multiplying, never quitting. That is eternity. What then is one thousand years? Time is relative; it has no span to God. But this is not so to man. Man measures time by days and years, and he walks minute by minute throughout the day, all 365 days of the year. Therefore, time stretches on and on to him. But to God, who is eternal, it takes one thousand years to make a day. Therefore, to ask why Jesus Christ has not yet returned after two thousand years is ridiculous. To God it has only been about two days since Christ died and arose. Two thousand years may seem like a long time to man, but not to God. To God, two days is only a drop in a bucket.

The point is this: believers must not be discouraged because Christ has not yet returned. God may want a lot more to take place on earth before He sends Christ back to earth. Our task is not to question when He is returning, but to watch and be ready in case He returns before we depart this life and go to Him.

2. There is the *intensity of time*. Note that one day with God is *as a thousand years*. Picture one day on the earth and consider...

- all the trials and temptations
- all the suffering and pain
- all the accidents and diseases
- all the sin and evil
- all the cursing and blasphemy against God
- all the selfishness and hoarding while millions are in desperate need
- all the people dying and being sent to hell

God feels every ounce of all the events. He loves us; therefore He feels it all. He suffers along with us, and the intensity of His feeling is absolute. God is absolute and perfect; therefore He feels in an absolute and perfect sense. He suffers with us with such intensity that we could never even imagine the experience. This is what is meant by "one day is with the Lord as a thousand years." The feelings of one day are so intense that it feels like a thousand years. Whereas we bear only the sufferings of our own personal experience, God bears the sufferings of all the experiences of *all men*. Therefore, to God the experience during just one day of an evil earth is as a thousand years to Him.

This point is significant: it is a warning to man. God will not bear evil forever. He will not suffer the rejection and rebellion of men too long. He will speak the Word and send Christ back to judge the world. Scripture definitely teaches that we are living in the last days.

> **"This know also, that in the last days perilous times shall come. For men shall be lovers of their own selves, covetous, boasters, proud, blasphemers, disobedient to parents, unthankful, unholy, without natural affection, trucebreakers, false accusers, incontinent, fierce, despisers of those that are good, traitors, heady, highminded, lovers of pleasures more than lovers of God; having a form of godliness, but denying the power thereof: from such turn away"** (2 Tim.3:1-5).

ILLUSTRATION:
Waiting on the Lord is something that requires great patience. Listen to this man's understanding of why God takes so long to do things.

> *Max was a carpenter's helper who understood the need to put quality in his work. His employer had the reputation of building the finest homes in his town. It was not unusual for his crew to finish a job weeks after the builders from other companies had moved on to other jobs. Max's boss was a stickler for the details that other carpenters ignored.*
>
> *One day Max became discouraged about how long it was taking to finish a house. But while eating lunch, he reflected back on a lesson his Sunday school teacher had taught. Max remembered that Jesus was also a carpenter who took His time because He was a stickler for the details that others ignored. After he finished his sandwich, it suddenly dawned on him: If it has taken Jesus almost 2,000 years to build my mansion, it must be too wonderful to imagine!*

Jesus said,

> **"In My Father's house are many mansions: if it were not so, I would have told you. I go to prepare a place for you. And if I go and prepare a place for you, I will come again, and receive you unto Myself; that where I am, there ye may be also"** (Jn.14:2-3).

Are you patiently waiting for the return of Jesus Christ?

QUESTIONS:
1. Think about a thousand years being as one day. If you should be God, would you be in a hurry to end the world? Why or why not?
2. Imagine how deeply God's heart must be cut as He waits to return to earth, how much pain He must feel because of the terrible evil, cursing, and suffering that go on every day all around the earth. Does it help you to endure the little suffering you do in comparison? How does His patience confirm His love for you?

2. THE LORD IS NOT SLOW IN SENDING CHRIST BACK TO EARTH, BUT IS LONGSUFFERING (v.9).

Why has Christ not yet returned to earth? Because God loves man; He does not want any person to perish, not a single person. God is not slack in fulfilling His promise nor is He powerless to return and judge the earth. He has not returned for one reason and one reason only. He wants more and more people to come to repentance. Note two significant points.

1. God is longsuffering. The word means...
   - God is patient with us.
   - God bears and suffers a long time with us.
   - God perseveres and is constant in suffering with us.
   - God is stedfast and enduring in being patient with us.

Very simply, God is slow to give in and to judge and condemn us. God loves and cares for us despite our sin and rebellion, cursing and rejection. This is the very reason He sent Christ to save us. He loves and cares for us; therefore, He is suffering a long time with us.

> "And the times of this ignorance God winked at; but now commandeth all men every where to repent: because he hath appointed a day, in the which he will judge the world in righteousness by that man whom he hath ordained; whereof he hath given assurance unto all men, in that he hath raised him from the dead" (Acts 17:30-31).

2. God wants no person to perish. To perish is a terrible thing. It means to be utterly lost and destroyed. It means to lose eternal life and to be cut off from life forever and ever. It means to be spiritually destitute, completely empty of all good. It means to suffer the judgment, condemnation, and punishment of separation from God forever and ever. It means to perish; to be in a state of suffering forever and ever apart from God.

The point is this: God does not want us perishing; He does not want us cut off and separated from Him. God wants us to spend eternity with Him not apart from Him.

> "For God so loved the world, that he gave his only begotten Son, that whosoever believeth in him should not perish, but have everlasting life" (Jn.3:16).

3. God wants all to come to repentance (see A CLOSER LOOK, Repentance-- 2 Pt.3:9 for discussion).

QUESTIONS:
1. In what ways has God been longsuffering toward you? Are you as longsuffering with others? Should you be?
2. What is God's attitude toward the lost? How should His attitude compel you to share the gospel?
3. Is there anything on earth worth perishing for? How does a person know for sure he will not perish?

A CLOSER LOOK:

(3:9) **Repentance**: to change; to turn; to change one's mind; to turn one's life. It is a turning away from sin and turning to God. It is a change of mind, a forsaking of sin. It is putting sin out of one's thoughts and behavior. It is resolving never to think or do a thing again. (Cp. Mt.3:2; Lk.13:2-3; Acts 2:38; 3:19; 8:22; 26:20.) The change is turning away from lying, stealing, cheating, immorality, cursing, drunkenness, and the other so-called glaring *sins of the flesh*. But the change is also turning away from *the silent sins of the spirit* such as self-centeredness, selfishness, envy, bitterness, pride, covetousness, anger, evil thoughts, hopelessness, laziness, jealousy, and lust.

1.   Repentance involves two turns. There is a negative turn away from sin and a positive turn toward God. It is a turning *to* God *away* from sin, whether sins of thought or action.

2.   Repentance is more than sorrow. Sorrow may or may not be involved in repentance. A person may repent simply because he wills and acts to change, or a person may repent because he senses an agonizing sorrow within. But the sense or feeling of sorrow is not repentance. Repentance is both the change of mind and the actual turning of one's life away from sin and toward God.

   "And saying, Repent ye: for the kingdom of heaven is at hand"
   (Mt.3:2).

QUESTIONS:
1. What does true repentance involve? Is there anything you need to repent of to-day?
2. What would be an example of feeling sorrow? Of true repentance?
3. Why is it not sufficient to just have sorrow?

3. THE DAY OF THE LORD IS COMING (v.10).

Why has Christ not yet returned to earth? The glorious fact is that He shall return. The Day of the Lord is coming. He is going to bring about the glorious day of redemption, giving all believers the wonderful privilege of living with Him forever and ever.

1.   The day of the Lord will come as a thief in the night. Note a significant fact: a man never knows when a thief is going to hit his house. No thief tells a man ahead of time that he is going to strike his house. If a man knew, he would watch and prepare. This is just the point: the Lord Jesus Christ has told us that He is coming back to earth. He has forewarned us, but He has not told us when. Why?

⇒ Not knowing when Jesus is returning keeps us focused upon Him and His return. It keeps us looking and longing for Him. It keeps us watching, and it stirs us to live pure and holy lives.

⇒ Not knowing when Jesus is returning serves as a warning to unbelievers. It warns them that they must repent now, today, for He could return today and catch them unprepared.

The day of the Lord is coming, but it is coming as a thief in the night. His return is going to be totally unexpected by most people. The believer must...
•   not be careless: get tired of waiting up, get sleepy, be caught off guard, begin to disbelieve. (All of this can happen to a houseowner waiting on a burglar.)
•   watch: sit up, stay awake, listen, look, take notice of all noises and sights (signs). (The burglar always comes in an unexpected hour.)

"Watch ye therefore: for ye know not when the master of the house cometh, at even, or at midnight, or at the cockcrowing, or in the morning" (Mk.13:35).

ILLUSTRATION:

The Lord *is* returning, and the believer needs to live each day as though He is coming that day. The urgency of the moment compels us to share the gospel with a keen awareness of the times. Making the decision to share the gospel NOW is critically important.

"*One morning the young new president of a bank made an appointment with his predecessor to seek some advice. He began, 'Sir, as you well know, I lack a great deal of the qualifications you already have for this job. You have been successful as president of this bank, and I wondered if you would be kind enough to share with me some of the insights you have gained from your years here that have been the keys to your success.'*

"*The older man looked at him with a stare and replied: 'Young man, two words: good decisions.'*

"*The young man responded, 'Thank you very much, sir, but how does one come to know which is the good decision?'*

"'*One word, young man: experience.'*

"'*But how does one get experience?'*

"'*Two words, young man: bad decisions.'*"[1]

Time is too precious to make bad decisions about eternity. We've a story to tell to the nations. As each day passes, we find ourselves one day shorter than before.

2. The heavens and universe shall pass away: all "the elements shall melt with fervent heat, the earth also and the works that are therein." Based upon what we know about the universe today--the basic elements such as the atom--nothing really needs to be said about how the universe is going to be destroyed. It is rather a matter of belief in God, that God is God, the Supreme Intelligence and Force of the universe. If a person believes in God, then he knows that God can destroy the universe. How? By doing what He did when He created the world and when He destroyed the earth the first time (cp. v.5-6), that is, by simply speaking the Word, by simply commanding a universal atomic explosion to take place.

Man himself has enough intelligence to burst the atom and to cause a chain reaction that would be so devastating it would destroy the earth and melt the elements of the earth with fervent heat. Man himself can cause an explosion so severe that every element of the earth would melt with fervent heat. Why, then, doubt God?

All God has to do is speak the Word and all the atoms throughout the universe will burn up in a chain reaction. There would be an atomic explosion that would destroy the whole universe.

The point is this: "the day of the Lord will come." There is no question about it.

⇒ Just as God spoke the Word and created the world...

⇒ just as God spoke the Word and destroyed the earth in Noah's day...

⇒ so God is going to speak the Word and the day of the Lord will come.

"**The heavens shall pass away with a great noise, and the elements shall melt with fervent heat, the earth also and the works that are therein shall be burned up**" (v.10).

---

[1] Michael P. Green. *Illustrations for Biblical Preaching*, p.396.

Now note: Why is God going to destroy both heaven and earth? There is one glorious reason and verse thirteen tells us: so He can create a new heavens and earth where righteousness dwells. God wants a perfect world in which there will be nothing but righteousness. Note: verse ten says that the earth and "the works that are therein shall be burned up." By "works" is meant all the works of man's hands:

⇒ services   ⇒ buildings
⇒ evil works   ⇒ offices
⇒ businesses   ⇒ houses
⇒ murder   ⇒ religion
⇒ wars   ⇒ governments

Everything man has ever done, all of his corruptible works, shall be burned up and destroyed by the fire of God's judgment. The whole universe will be destroyed by fire; a fiery explosion will take place and the fire will be so hot that every element will melt from the fervent heat. But note: it is all so that God's eternal purpose for the universe can be fulfilled. God is going to create a new heavens and earth in which only righteousness will exist. The righteous, those who have trusted the Lord Jesus Christ for righteousness, shall be the citizens of the new heavens and earth. The new heavens and earth will be the home where God's people will live and serve Him for all eternity.

APPLICATION:

What man must do is watch and prepare. He must repent, turn to God, and turn away from his sin and the coming destruction. Scripture is clear, and it is stated as clearly as it can be.

"For verily I say unto you, Till heaven and earth pass, one jot or one tittle shall in no wise pass from the law, till all be fulfilled" (Mt.5:18).

QUESTIONS:

1. Have you ever been burglarized? Were you prepared? If you had been more alert, what would have done differently?
2. As a believer, what is your responsibility in preparing for Christ's return? How can you convey the urgency to unbelievers?
3. Are you looking forward to the new heavens and earth? Why or why not?

SUMMARY:

Why has Christ not yet returned to earth? What you sense in your heart is not unknown to the Father. He is counting down the time and will say to His Son one day--RETURN! Until He does return, you can encourage yourself with these timely reminders...

1. The Lord does not measure time the same as man.
2. The Lord is not slow in sending Christ back to earth, but is longsuffering.
3. The Day of the Lord is coming.

PERSONAL JOURNAL NOTES:
(Reflection & Response)

1. The most important thing that I learned from this lesson was:

2. The thing that I need to work on the most is:

3. I can apply this lesson to my life by:

4. Closing Prayer of Commitment: (put your commitment down on paper).

	C. The Things Believers Must Do Since Jesus Christ is Coming Again (Part I), 3:11-14	heavens being on fire shall be dissolved, and the elements shall melt with fervent heat?	
1. Believers must live holy & godly lives	11 Seeing then that all these things shall be dissolved, what manner of persons ought ye to be in all holy conversation and godliness,	13 Nevertheless we, according to his promise, look for new heavens and a new earth, wherein dwelleth righteousness.	3. Believers must look for the new heavens & new earth
2. Believers must look for & speed up the Day of God	12 Looking for and hasting unto the coming of the day of God, wherein the	14 Wherefore, beloved, seeing that ye look for such things, be diligent that ye may be found of him in peace, without spot, and blameless.	4. Believers must be prepared for the coming of Christ a. Must be found in peace b. Must be spotless c. Must be blameless

Section III
THE COMING AGAIN OF CHRIST
AND THE END OF THE WORLD
2 Peter 3:1-18

Study 3: **THE THINGS BELIEVERS MUST DO SINCE JESUS CHRIST IS COMING AGAIN (PART I)**

Text: **2 Peter 3:11-14**

Aim: To carefully prepare for Christ's coming.

Memory Verse:
> "Nevertheless we, according to his promise, look for new heavens and a new earth, wherein dwelleth righteousness" (2 Peter 3:13).

INTRODUCTION:
Have you ever had to move? Do you remember all you had to do?
⇒ You had to pack all your possessions.
⇒ You had to make decisions about what to keep and what to discard.
⇒ You had to live out of boxes until you made the move.
⇒ You had to find some people to help you move.
⇒ You had to unpack and figure out where to place everything in your new home.

The moving experience is really a paradox: you look forward to moving into your new home, but the physical and emotional energy required--the stress that it brings--almost causes you to dread the move. But once you get everything unpacked and settled in, your new home can finally be enjoyed.

Likewise, there are many people who want to enjoy heaven but do not want to do the preparation necessary to get there. Preparing to move to heaven requires preparation on our part. Christ has done His part, but why is our part important in preparing to move? Because no one knows when we are going to move, to be taken by Christ to heaven. His

88

instructions are simple: "Be packed and ready to go at a moment's notice. Make certain all your affairs are in order. There will be *no* exceptions to this order."

Why is this such an important study? It is important because Jesus Christ is coming to earth again. Therefore, there are some things believers must do, and they are of critical importance.

OUTLINE:
1. Believers must live holy and godly lives (v.11).
2. Believers must look for and speed up the day of God (v.12).
3. Believers must look for the new heavens and new earth (v.13).
4. Believers must be prepared for the coming of Christ (v.14).

1. BELIEVERS MUST LIVE HOLY AND GODLY LIVES (v.11).

In fact, note the Scripture: *all of our behavior* must be holy and godly. There is to be no area of our lives--no part, no act--that is not holy and godly. Why? Why such a stress upon holiness and godliness? One strong reason is given.

The heavens and earth are to be dissolved because of the sin and evil of man. It is the sin and evil of man that has made the world so corrupt--corrupt beyond repair. God will be forced to destroy the world because of our sin and evil. The sin and evil of man has put the world under a curse of destruction. Sin and evil are therefore terrible things, abominable things! They should be hated and despised by every man, woman, and child. All sin and evil should be despised because of the terrible things they do and have done. They have caused a curse of corruption and utter destruction upon the earth. For this reason, we should hate sin and evil and love holiness and godliness. We should be holy and godly in all of our behavior.

1. *Holy* means that our behavior is sanctified, that is, set apart unto God; separated from the world and given over to God; given over to live pure and righteous lives.

> **"For I am the Lord that bringeth you up out of the land of Egypt, to be your God: ye shall therefore be holy, for I am holy" (Lev.11:45).**

2. *Godliness* means that we live like God and seek to be a godly person; that we live and do all things in the reverence and awe of God; that we are so conscious of God's presence that we live like God would live if He were walking upon earth (2 Pt.1:3).

APPLICATION:
Note: godliness means to be *Christ-like*. It is living upon earth just as Christ lived.

> **"But we all, with open face beholding as in a glass the glory of the Lord, are changed into the same image from glory to glory, even as by the Spirit of the Lord" (2 Cor.3:18).**

ILLUSTRATION:
Do you live a holy and godly life? As you journey through this life, you have been charged to produce the evidence of being a believer.

> *"Gustav Dore, the famous artist, lost his passport while traveling in Europe. He was at a certain boundary post between two countries and the officer in charge asked him for his passport. Dore fumbled about and finally announced, 'I*

have lost my passport, but it is all right. I'm Dore, the artist. Please let me go in.'

"The officer replied, 'Oh, no. We have plenty of people representing them-selves as this or that great person! Here is a pencil and paper. Now, if you are Dore, the artist, prove it by drawing me a picture!'*

"Dore took the pencil and drew some pictures of scenes in the immediate area.

"'Now, I am perfectly sure that you are Dore. No one else could draw like that!' said the officer as he allowed the great artist to enter the country.

"So it is with professing followers of Christ. You say you are a Christian. But can you really produce evidence?"[1]

QUESTIONS:
1. How can you live a holy and godly life in an evil and corrupt world? Why do some believers ignore this command of God?
2. Whom do you most admire for their godly lifestyle? What traits do they have?
3. What role do you have in cultivating holiness and godliness in your life? What is God's role? Are these traits an option?

2. BELIEVERS MUST LOOK FOR AND SPEED UP THE DAY OF GOD (v.12).

The day of God refers to the day when God shall dissolve and destroy the heavens and earth, the day when the universe "shall be set aflame by fire and shall be dissolved, and the elements shall melt with fervent heat" (v.12). What is to be the attitude of the believer toward the *day of God*?

1.   The believer is to be "looking for" the day of God. The word means to wait; to wait patiently but expectantly; to eagerly anticipate and long for the day of God; to be in expectation.[2]

2.   The believer is to *hasten* the day of God. The word "hastening" can mean two things.

　　a. *To hasten* can mean to hurry after; to earnestly desire; to rush toward. The be-liever is to live a holy and godly life looking for and hastening toward the day of God. Keeping his eyes upon that terrible day of judgment is to *arouse him* to live a holy and godly life. Every day he lives upon earth is to be a day in which he hastens toward the judgment of God; he should never take his eyes off the terri-ble day of God that is coming. If he takes his eyes off that day, if he fails to di-rect his life toward the day of God, then he will most likely slip into unholiness and ungodliness. He must, therefore, stay focused upon the day of God, the day of the terrible judgment to come upon the heavens and earth.

　　b. *To hasten* can also mean to *hasten on* the day of God; to rush the coming of Christ; to cause the day of God to come sooner. The believer has a part in bringing about the eternal kingdom of God; he has a part in bringing about the return of Christ and the great day of God. How? God is "longsuffering...not willing that any should perish" (v.9). This is the reason He is delaying the return of Christ. Apparently, God has a certain number of believers He has ordained to be brothers and sisters of His dear Son; apparently, there are to be a certain number of believers to rule and manage the new heavens and earth for Christ. In His eternal knowledge God certainly knows the number who will be saved and serving His dear Son. Whatever the number and whatever the case, that number

---

[1]   *Power.* Walter B. Knight. *Knight's Master Book of 4,000 Illustrations*, p.72.
[2]   W.E. Vine. *Expository Dictionary of New Testament Words.* (Old Tappan, NJ: Fleming H. Revell Co.).

has to be reached before Christ can come and before the great day of God can destroy the universe and make a new heavens and earth. This much is known for sure:

⇒ God does have a certain number of believers in mind. Being God, He has purposed that His Son have many brothers who will reign with Him and who will worship and serve God through all eternity (cp. Ro.8:28-29 where God will allow nothing to stop Him from giving Christ "many brothers.")

⇒ This Scripture tells us that we are to *hasten* on, to help bring about the day of God.

APPLICATION:

How can we help the day of God to come? How can we quicken the return of Christ and the end of the world? By living more holy and godly lives so that more people will more readily be attracted to Christ. The more they see *Christ in us*, His presence and power carrying us through the trials and temptations of life, the more they are going to want Christ and His power in their lives. The more holy and godly we live, the more people will see the things for which they long...

- strength to conquer the trials and temptations of life
- hope in the future
- assurance and confidence of living forever
- conviction, purpose, meaning, and significance in life
- love, joy, and peace

When people see these things, the things for which they long, they will be attracted to Christ much quicker. The result will be more souls for Christ. They will be won much quicker and the number that God has in mind will be reached much sooner. Therefore, the way we are to *speed up* the day of God is to live more dynamic lives for Christ. We must live more holy and godly lives for Christ, and we must witness more diligently than ever before. We must begin to tell everyone that the Messiah, the Savior of the world, has come--that He has come to save us from the sin and death of the world and to give us a life of love, joy, peace, and power-- the power to live abundantly both now and forever.

> "For the hope which is laid up for you in heaven, whereof ye heard before in the word of the truth of the gospel; which is come unto you, as it is in all the world; and bringeth forth fruit, as it doth also in you, since the day ye heard of it, and knew the grace of God in truth" (Col.1:5-6).

QUESTIONS:

1. Are you living in such a way that you are *hastening* toward the "day of God"? Does your lifestyle show that you care more about this world than the world to come? If so, when do you plan to change?
2. How can you actually help the day of God come? Have you been doing your part?
3. Should speeding up the day of the Lord not be the desire of every believer's heart?

3. BELIEVERS MUST LOOK FOR THE NEW HEAVENS AND NEW EARTH (v.13).

Scripture clearly says that God is going to create a new heavens and a new earth. No matter what men may think and say about the issue, God declares as simply and as clearly as human language can describe that He is going to make a *new heavens and a new earth*. Why? So that the world will be perfect and nothing but righteousness will exist therein. God has *ordained* a perfect world, a world in which only righteous people will live. God wants a world where there will be no more sin and evil, no more accidents, disease, suffering, murder, drunkenness, drugs, adultery, sexual perversion, war, or death. God wants a people who know only the fulness of love, joy, and peace, a people who worship and serve Him forever and ever. The great Biblical commentator Matthew Henry says:

> *"In these new heavens and earth...only righteousness shall dwell; this is to be the habitation of such righteous persons as do righteousness, and are free from the power and pollution of sin...those only who are clothed with the righteousness of Christt, and sanctified by the Holy Ghost, shall be admitted to dwell in this holy place."*[3]

> **"For I reckon that the sufferings of this present time are not worthy to be compared with the glory which shall be revealed in us. For the earnest expectation of the creature [creation] waiteth for the manifestation of the sons of God. For the creature was made subject to vanity, not willingly, but by reason of him who hath subjected the same in hope. Because the creature itself also shall be delivered from the bondage of corruption into the glorious liberty of the children of God. For we know that the whole creation groaneth and travaileth in pain together until now" (Ro.8:18-22).**

QUESTIONS:
1. Why do men deny that God will create a new heavens and a new earth? Does their denial have any effect on the truth?
2. Imagine what life will be like in the new heavens and new earth. No sin, evil, disease, war, and on and on. Would you ever want to go back to life on this earth? What impact should this have on your Christian witness now?

4. BELIEVERS MUST BE PREPARED FOR THE COMING OF CHRIST (v.14).

The word "diligent" means to be eager; to strive earnestly; to be zealous in seeking after. The believer is to be diligent, that is, eager, earnest and zealous in preparing himself for the return of the Lord. Why? So the Lord will find him prepared. Note that three preparations are necessary.

1. The believer must be found in *peace*. He must be at peace with *both God and man*. He must not be living in rebellion against God nor be divided against his brothers and sisters. He must not be...
- living like he wants instead of how God says
- doing his own thing
- disobeying God
- living in sin
- cheating, lying, or stealing
- being selfish and hateful
- gossiping and criticizing
- grumbling and backbiting
- stirring up trouble within the church
- neglecting and ignoring God

---

[3] *Matthew Henry's Commentary, Vol.6.* (Old Tappan, NJ: Fleming H. Revell), p.105.

The believer must be at peace with God and with men. He must be living just like God says to live, and he must be living as one with his brothers and sisters. When Christ comes, no believer dare be found criticizing and being divided from a brother or sister. And no believer dare be found at odds with Christ and not living for Christ. Such sinful behavior will be severely judged.

> **"Therefore being justified by faith, we have peace with God through our Lord Jesus Christ" (Ro.5:1).**

2. The believer must be *without spot*. This means to be clean, pure, and unsoiled; to have no dirt, pollution, or contamination of sin whatsoever. The believer is to be confessing his sins always, all day long. He is to be walking in constant communion and fellowship with Christ, walking in open confession, confessing all the sin and contamination that he picks up from the world. Just being in the world means that some of the pollution of sin catches the eye and ears of the believer and causes unclean thoughts to cross his mind. The believer must walk in open confession, praying always for the power of Christ's blood to cleanse him and to keep him pure. This is the only way a believer can ever be found spotless by Christ when He returns.

> **"If we confess our sins, he is faithful and just to forgive us our sins, and to cleanse us from all unrighteousness" (1 Jn.1:9).**

3. The believer must be found *blameless*. The word means free from fault and censure, above reproach and rebuke. The believer is to live a blameless, faultless, and pure life, both in the church and in the world. No one is to be able to point to the Christian and accuse or blame him with anything. The Christian is to be clean, unpolluted, spotless, holy, righteous, and pure before man and God.

> **"They ye may be blameless and harmless, the sons of God, without rebuke, in the midst of a crooked and perverse nation, among whom ye shine as lights in the world" (Ph.2:15).**
> **"Now unto him that is able to keep you from falling, and to present you faultless before the presence of his glory with exceeding joy" (Jude 24).**

ILLUSTRATION:
You must be ready for the Lord's return. You must prepare for His return with all diligence.

> *"Lord Joseph Duveen, American head of the art firm that bore his name, planned in 1915 to send one of his experts to England to examine some ancient pottery. He booked passage on the Lusitania. Then the German Embassy issued a warning that the liner might be torpedoed. Duveen wanted to call off the trip. 'I can't take the risk of your being killed,' he said to his young employee.*
> *"'Don't worry,' said the man, 'I'm a strong swimmer, and when I read what was happening in the Atlantic, I began hardening myself by spending time every day in a tub of ice water. At first I could sit only a few minutes, but this morning, I stayed in that tub nearly two hours.'*
> *"Naturally, Duveen laughed. It sounded preposterous. But his expert sailed, and the Lusitania was torpedoed. The young man was rescued after nearly five hours in the chilly ocean, still in excellent condition.*

*"Just as this young man did, so Christians should condition them-
selves by practicing devotional discipline, behavioral discipline, and
discipline in doing good."[4]*

When Jesus Christ returns to this earth, will you be ready? How well you prepare
now determines the outcome!

QUESTIONS:

1. If you are already saved, why is it so important to prepare yourself for the
   Lord's return?
2. Realistically, how can you be faultless, blameless, and spotless on *any* day, much
   less every day until Christ returns?
3. Are you confident you are doing all you can to prepare for the coming of Christ?

SUMMARY:

When the call comes to move from this earth to the Promised Land of heaven, will you
be ready? Take time now and prepare yourself for Christ's coming. Those who want to
be ready will...

1. Live holy and godly lives.
2. Look for and speed up the day of God.
3. Look for the new heavens and new earth.
4. Be prepared for the coming of Christ.

PERSONAL JOURNAL NOTES:
(Reflection & Response)

1. The most important thing that I learned from this lesson was:

2. The thing that I need to work on the most is:

3. I can apply this lesson to my life by:

4. Closing Prayer Of Commitment: (put your commitment down on paper).

---

[4] Cited in *Christianity Today*, *February 1979, p.25*. Michael P. Green. *Illustrations for
Biblical Preaching*, p.109-110.

D. The Things Believers Must Do Since Jesus Christ is Coming Again (Part II), 3:15-18		
1. Believers must count the Lord's longsuffering as salvation a. God is working to save more & more people b. Paul confirms the same point c. Some twist the Scriptures to their own destruction	derstood, which they that are unlearned and unstable wrest, as they do also the other scriptures, unto their own destruction. 17 Ye therefore, beloved, seeing ye know these things before, beware lest ye also, being led away with the error of the wicked, fall from your own stedfastness. 18 But grow in grace, and in the knowledge of our Lord and Saviour Jesus Christ. To him be glory both now and for ever. Amen.	2. Believers must beware lest they be led into error 3. Believers must grow in the grace & knowledge of our Lord

(Text in middle column verses 15-16:) 15 And account that the longsuffering of our Lord is salvation; even as our beloved brother Paul also according to the wisdom given unto him hath written unto you; 16 As also in all his epistles, speaking in them of these things; in which are some things hard to be un-

Section III
THE COMING AGAIN OF CHRIST
AND THE END OF THE WORLD
2 Peter 3:1-18

Study 4: **THE THINGS BELIEVERS MUST DO SINCE JESUS CHRIST IS COMING AGAIN**

Text: **2 Peter 3:15-18**

Aim: To reinforce your commitment to Christ, your commitment to live a more godly life until Christ returns.

Memory Verse:
> "But grow in grace, and in the knowledge of our Lord and Saviour Jesus Christ. To him be glory both now and for ever" (2 Peter 3:18).

INTRODUCTION:

Have you ever waited for someone to meet you at a restaurant...and waited...and waited? As you glanced at your watch and cut your eye toward the entrance, the waiting seemed to turn into a contest of endurance. Did you get tired of waiting and leave, or did you patiently wait for your party to join you? Every day people miss important and unique opportunities because they are unwilling to wait a moment longer. Think of all the...

- business deals
- times of laughter
- rich moments of fellowship

...that are missed. Think of the time that is spent fussing and fuming instead of praying and meditating--all because people run out of patience. Relative to these examples is a far greater reason for waiting. God has charged each believer to live in an expectant frame of mind, waiting for the Lord's return.

As you wait for the Lord's return, are you ready for His call to move out, to move on to heaven? The marching orders from the previous study are still in effect: "Be packed and ready to go at a moment's notice. Make certain all your affairs are in order."

This passage concludes the second letter of Peter. The emphasis of this concluding exhortation is striking. Jesus Christ is coming again, but His coming has been delayed. Believers are still on earth waiting for Him to come. What then are we to be doing? There are some critical things we should be doing. What are they? (Note: this is a continuation of the former passage and subject, 2 Pt.3:11-14.)

OUTLINE:
1. Believers must count the Lord's longsuffering as salvation (v.15-16).
2. Believers must beware lest they be led into error (v.17).
3. Believers must grow in the grace and knowledge of our Lord (v.18).

1. BELIEVERS MUST COUNT THE LORD'S LONGSUFFERING AS SALVATION (v.15-16).

1. Remember: scoffers ridicule the coming again of Jesus Christ. They say such is foolishness. They say that the world is operated and run by the natural laws of nature; they say that if God existed and cared about the world, He would have come long ago and saved the world from all the evil, corruption, murder, and war that rages on and on (v.3-4). Remember what Scripture says, why it is that Jesus Christ has not yet come: because God is longsuffering and does not want any person to perish. He wants all to repent and to be saved (v.9). Now note: this is what the present verse is referring to. We are to count the longsuffering of God as salvation. The Lord Jesus has not yet returned to earth for one reason and one reason only: that more and more people might be saved, that more and more might be snatched out of the claws of death and judgment. This is the reason the Lord delays His return. His delay...
- is not because He has forgotten the earth.
- is not because He is angry with man because man has not paid more attention to His Word and teaching.
- is not because He does not care and love man enough to deliver him out of the evil, corruption, and suffering of the world.

The Lord cares and loves man so much that He wants all men to be saved. He longs for *all men* to repent and turn to Him. He shrinks from the thought of returning because He knows that when He returns every single unbeliever is doomed forever and ever. Therefore, He waits one more day; He waits longing for a few more to be saved; He waits because He knows that all unbelievers will be doomed to judgment and destruction.

The point is this: the believer must count the longsuffering of the Lord as salvation, as His concern for souls. We must never look upon the Lord's delay as unconcern or lack of care for His people and for the world. God loves all people, every single person on earth; therefore, He is longsuffering with the sin and evil of men. He is suffering a long time with man and his cursing and rebellion and rejection. But the day will come when God cannot bear sin and evil any longer. When that day comes, He will return and all the unbelievers and ungodly of this world will fall into the hands of an angry God, a God who is just and holy and righteous--just as much so as He is loving and longsuffering and caring.

2. Note a significant fact: Peter says that Paul wrote the same thing in his writings. That is, Paul taught that God delayed the coming of Christ so that more and more people could be saved.

> **"Being justified freely by his grace through the redemption that is in Christ Jesus: whom God hath set forth to be a propitiation through faith in his blood, to declare his righteousness for the re-**

mission of sins that are past, through the forbearance [long-suffering] of God" (Ro.3:24-25).

3.   Note that some people twist the Scripture to their viewpoint. The point is this: believers are not to take the delay of Christ and assume that it is going to be years and years before He ever comes, before we have to face judgment. We must keep our eyes on His return, watch, prepare, and be ready at all times. If we are not watching, then we are being lazy and complacent and are much more likely to fall into sin and worldliness. And if this happens, we will be caught unprepared and be spotted, dirtied with sin, and stand blamable before Him (cp. v.14).

The Lord is not delaying His return so we can enjoy this world and its pleasures and possessions more. This earth is to be dissolved, utterly destroyed, and melted down. The Lord is delaying His return because He is longsuffering, wanting more and more people to be saved. Our task is to be more evangelistic; to live more spotless and blameless lives so that we can reach more and more people for Christ. The delay of Christ should not cause us to become lethargic, complacent, and worldly; it should stir us to be more diligent in the mission of Christ. If we twist the Scripture, allowing the longsuffering of God to stir the thought that we have a little more time to wait, then we are destroying ourselves.

"Jesus answered and said unto them, Ye do err, not knowing the scriptures, nor the power of God" (Mt.22:29).

APPLICATION:

Note two things.

1) Peter said that Paul wrote some things that were difficult to understand. He also says some people twisted what Paul said just as they twisted the truth of God's longsuffering. What were those things?
    ⇒ Paul's teaching on justification by faith. This teaching led some people to say that when a person believed in Christ, he was saved no matter how he lived. Even if a person lived like the devil himself, if he believed in Christ, he was saved. This, of course, leads to the abuse of grace (cp. Ro.3:5-8; 6:1f; Jas.2:14-26).
    ⇒ Paul's teaching on Christian liberty and freedom. This teaching led some people to say that Paul was removing the restrictions of God upon behavior and giving license to live and do as one likes (Ro.8:1-2; 7:4; 14:1-23; 1 Cor.6:12; Gal.3:10; 5:13).
2) Peter said that Paul's writings were accepted as Scripture by the early church (v.16). He says that they twisted Paul's writings even as they did "the other Scriptures."

QUESTIONS:
1. How would you answer the scoffer's charges that the second coming of Christ is foolish?
2. What is God's attitude toward those who have yet to give their hearts to Him? How can you make this attitude yours also?
3. What should be the believer's outlook on the delay of Christ's return? In what ways can you make the best use of your time as you wait for His return?

2. BELIEVERS MUST BEWARE LEST THEY BE LED INTO ERROR (v.17).

Note that Peter addresses the believers of the churches as *beloved*. He loves God's people, and it has been his love that has stirred him to warn them of the great day of God that is coming, the terrible judgment and destruction of the ungodly and of the heavens and earth. Now Peter gives the *beloved* believers one more warning:

> **"Ye therefore, beloved, seeing ye know these things before, beware lest ye also, being led away with the error of the wicked, fall from your own stedfastness" (v.17).**

The believer has been warned; he now knows all about these things. He has read and studied the letter of Second Peter...

- the message of the great love and salvation of God, of the coming judgment of God upon man and his world.
- the message that warns against false teachers who pervert and twist the Scriptures. They deny the Lord (2 Pt.2:1f) and the Scripture (2 Pt.2:1f), the return of Christ, and the judgment to come (2 Pt.3:3f).

The believer has been warned; therefore, he must now beware, guard and stand against the error of false teachers. If he does not stay alert and guard against the teaching of false teachers, he will be led away by their error. The believer will fall and no longer be stedfast. He will lose the exciting hope of the Lord's return and no longer look forward to the glorious union with Christ nor to eternal life with God the Father.

> **"Watch and pray, that ye enter not into temptation: the spirit indeed is willing, but the flesh is weak" (Mt.26:41).**

ILLUSTRATION:

The Christian believer is without excuse when it comes to knowing the truth. God has given His Word, the Holy Bible, and the Holy Spirit to guide the believer into the truth. Once you know the truth, it is your duty to act upon it. Here is a stirring story that will encourage you to practice what you know.

> *"You probably have heard played many times 'The Stars and Stripes Forever,' a spirited march by John Phillip Sousa. Sitting in his hotel room one summer evening, Mr. Sousa heard a hand organ man in the street below playing this, his favorite march, in a slow, dragging manner. He dashed to the street. 'Here, here,' he called to the sleepy, lazy grinder, 'that is no way to play that march!'*
>
> *"He seized the handle of the organ and turned it vigorously. The music rushed out, spirited and snappy. The hand organ man bowed low and smiled. The next night Mr. Sousa heard the organ again. This time the tempo was right. Looking out the window, he saw a great crowd gathering about the player. Over the organ on a large card was the grinder's name, and under it, 'Pupil of John Philip Sousa.'*
>
> *"The organ grinder was quick to put into practice what he had learned, and he was proud to have learned from such a great teacher....And you--are you ashamed to let it be known that you are a pupil of the Lord Jesus; and do you put into practice the things you learn of Him?"*[1]

You have learned the truth--now live it out!

QUESTIONS:

1. How is it possible for a believer to be led into error? What can you do to guard yourself from falling into error?
2. What can happen if you fail to stay alert and guard yourself against false teachers?
3. It is not sufficient just to know the truth without doing the truth. Why not? What happens if you have one without the other?

---

[1]   Walter B. Knight. *Knight's Master Book of 4,000 Illustrations*, p.440-441.

3. BELIEVERS MUST GROW IN THE GRACE AND KNOWLEDGE OF OUR LORD (v.18).

Note the close of Peter's letter, a glorious exaltation of praise: "To Him be glory both now and forever." All the glory that belongs to God, Peter says belongs to Jesus Christ. And if any one person should know, Peter should. Peter is the *big fisherman*, the man chosen by Christ to be one of His closest associates, to be the leader of His small apostolic band. No one knew Jesus Christ any better than Peter. And Peter says that the glory due God belongs to Jesus Christ. Jesus Christ is God incarnate in human flesh, God who came down to earth to reveal Himself and to save men.

Matthew Henry says:

> *"We must grow in the knowledge of our Lord Jesus Christ....so as to be more like him and to love him better. This is the knowledge of Christ the apostle Paul reached after and desired to attain, Ph.3:10. Such a knowledge of Christ as conforms us more to him and [will] preserve us from falling off in times of...apostasy; and those who experience...the knowledge of the Lord and Saviour Jesus Christ will...give thanks and praise to him, and join with our apostle in saying, To him be glory both now and for ever. Amen."[2]*

ILLUSTRATION:

The final thing you need to do before Jesus Christ comes again is give Him all the praise for saving you. Just think: those who love Him will live with Him forever! Author Max Lucado helps close these thoughts with this special insight into the grace of God.

> *"A fellow is doing some shopping at a commissary on a military base. Doesn't need much, just some coffee and a loaf of bread. He is standing in line at the checkout stand. Behind him is a woman with a full cart. Her basket overflows with groceries, clothing, and a VCR.*
> *"At his turn he steps up to the register. The clerk invites him to draw a piece of paper out of a fishbowl. 'If you pull out the correct slip, then all your groceries are free,' the clerk explains.*
> *"'How many 'correct slips' are there?' asks the buyer.*
> *"'Only one.'*
> *"The bowl is full so the chances are slim, but the fellow tries anyway, and wouldn't you know it, he gets the winning ticket! What a surprise. But then he realizes he is only buying coffee and bread. What a waste.*
> *"But this fellow is quick. He turns to the lady behind him--the one with the mountain of stuff--and proclaims, 'Well, what do you know, Honey? We won! We don't have to pay a penny.'*
> *"She stares at him. He winks at her. And somehow she has the wherewithal to play along. She steps up beside him. Puts her arm in his and smiles. And for a moment they stand side-by-side, wedded by good fortune. In the parking lot she consummates the temporary union with a kiss and a hug and goes her way with a grand story to tell her friends.*
> *"I know, I know. What they did was a bit shady. He shouldn't have lied and she shouldn't have pretended. But that taken into account, it's still a nice story.*
> *"A story not too distant from our own. We, too, have been graced with a surprise. Even more than that of the lady. For though her debt was high, she could pay it. We can't begin to pay ours.*

---

[2] *Matthew Henry's Commentary*, Vol.6, p.1059.

"We, like the woman, have been given a gift. Not just at the checkout stand, but at the judgment seat.

"And we, too, have become a bride. Not just for a moment, but for eternity. And not just for groceries, but for the feast. Don't we have a grand story to tell our friends?"[3]

Praise God, we do have a grand story to tell! Who will you tell today?

QUESTIONS:
1. How can you grow in the grace and knowledge of Jesus Christ? Why should you?
2. Who needs to receive all the glory for your salvation?
3. How can you show praise and thanksgiving to Christ for what He has done for you?

SUMMARY:

If Jesus Christ were to return today, would you be ready? How sad it would be if you were caught unprepared. God wants you ready and has given you specific instructions on how you are to prepare yourself:

1. You must remember that the Lord's longsuffering means salvation for more and more people.
2. You must beware lest you be led into error.
3. You must grow in the grace and knowledge of our Lord.

PERSONAL JOURNAL NOTES:
(Reflection & Response)

1. The most important thing that I learned from this lesson was:

2. The thing that I need to work on the most is:

3. I can apply this lesson to my life by:

4. Closing Prayer of Commitment: (put your commitment down on paper).

---

[3] Max Lucado. *When God Whispers Your Name*. (Dallas, TX: Word Publishing, 1994), p.71-72.

OUTLINE & SUBJECT INDEX

2 PETER

OUTLINE & SUBJECT INDEX

OUTLINE & SUBJECT INDEX

2 PETER

REMEMBER: When you look up a subject and turn to the Scripture reference, you have not only the Scripture, you have an outline and a discussion (commentary) of the Scripture and subject.

This is one of the GREAT VALUES of the Teacher's Outline & Study Bible. Once you have all the volumes, you will have not only what all other Bible indexes give you, that is, a list of all the subjects and their Scripture references, BUT you will also have...

- An outline of every Scripture and subject in the Bible.
- A discussion (commentary) on every Scripture and subject.
- Every subject supported by other Scriptures or cross references.

DISCOVER THE GREAT VALUE for yourself. Quickly glance below to the very first subject of the Index of First Peter. It is:

ABOUND
Meaning.   2 Pt.1:8-11

Turn to the reference. Glance at the Scripture and outline of the Scripture, then read the commentary. You will immediately see the GREAT VALUE of the INDEX of The Teacher's Outline & Study Bible.

OUTLINE AND SUBJECT INDEX

ABOUND
Meaning.   2 Pt.1:8-11

ADULTERY
Sin of. Trait of false teachers.   2 Pt.2:14

ANGELS
Power of. Greater than man's.   2 Pt.2:10-19

ANGELS, FALLEN
Fall of. Discussed.   2 Pt.2:4
Judgment of. Discussed.   2 Pt.2:4

APOSTASY
Danger - fate of.
Judgment.   2 Pt.2:1
The midst of darkness.   2 Pt.2:17; 2:10-22
Deliverance from. By going on to maturity.   2 Pt.1:10
Described as.
A time existing now. In the church now.   2 Pt.2:1-3; 2:10-22
A time in the future. The last times.   2 Pt.3:3

OUTLINE & SUBJECT INDEX

OUTLINE & SUBJECT INDEX

OUTLINE & SUBJECT INDEX

OUTLINE & SUBJECT INDEX

OUTLINE & SUBJECT INDEX

OUTLINE & SUBJECT INDEX

False s. How man seeks to meet his needs.	2 Pt.1:16
How men are s. By the longsuffering of God.	2 Pt.3:9; 3:15-16
Proof of.	
Discussed.	2 Pt.1:16-21; 1:16
Scripture.	2 Pt.1:19-21
Salvation in Second Peter.	
The great duties of s.	2 Pt.1:5-7
The great proof of s.	2 Pt.1:16-18
The great gift of Christ in s.	2 Pt.1:1-4
The great promises of s.	2 Pt.1:8-11
The great s. of God.	2 Pt.1:1-21
The great task of ministers in s.	2 Pt.1:12-15
Source - How one is s.	
Christ.	2 Pt.1:1-4
God's longsuffering.	2 Pt.3:8-15

SCOFFERS

Work of. Scoff at the return of Christ and the judgment of the world.	2 Pt.3:1-7; 3:8-10

SCRIPTURE

Books and contents of.	2 Pt.1:19-21
History of. Discussed.	2 Pt.1:19-21
Inspiration of.	
Given through the Holy Spirit.	2 Pt.1:21
Is not a fable.	2 Pt.1:16
Interpretation of. Not of private i.	2 Pt.1:20-21
Prophecies. Fulfilled. (See **PROPHECIES**)	
Proves salvation.	2 Pt.1:19-21

SELF-CONTROL

Meaning.	2 Pt.1:5-7

SERVANT

Discussed.	2 Pt.1:1

SIN

Duty. Not to turn back.	2 Pt.2:20-22
Result. Enslaves.	2 Pt.2:19

SODOM AND GOMORRHA

Destroyed by God.	2 Pt.2:6
Judgment of.	2 Pt.2:6

SPIRITUAL WORD

Disbelief in. Discussed.	2 Pt.2:10-12

SPOTLESS

Meaning.	2 Pt.3:14

OUTLINE & SUBJECT INDEX

TEACHERS, FALSE
    Behavior.
        Character and conduct.   2 Pt.2:10-22
        Discussed.   2 Pt.2:10-22
        Servants of corruption.   2 Pt.2:10-22
        Sins of.   2 Pt.2:11
    Contrasted with angels.   2 Pt.2:11
    Discussed. Description of.   2 Pt.1:9; 2:10-22
    Duty. Must beware of false teachers.   2 Pt.3:17
    Judgment of.   2 Pt.2:1; 2:3-9;
                                    2:20-22
    Life - Walk. Discussed.   2 Pt.2:10-22
    Message of. Deny the supernatural - scoff.   2 Pt.3:1-7
    Names - Titles. Servants of corruption.   2 Pt.2:19
    Results. Enslaves.   2 Pt.2:19
    Teaching of.
        A fable, a creation of their own mind.   2 Pt.1:16
        Deny the Lord.   2 Pt.2:1
        Most tragic teaching. Denial of the Lord.   2 Pt.2:1
        Teach contrary to God's Word.   2 Pt.2:1
        Teach heresy.   2 Pt.2:1
    Warning to. Discussed.   2 Pt.2:1; 2:3-9;
                                    2:20-22
    Where they are. In the church.   2 Pt.2:1
    Why they teach false doctrine. Discussed.   2 Pt.2:3

TEMPERANCE
    Meaning.   2 Pt.1:5-7

TEMPTATION (See **SIN; TRIALS**)
    Conquering - Deliverance. God knows how to deliver.   2 Pt.2:9

TESTIMONY
    The great eyewitness account of salvation.   2 Pt.1:16-18

TIME, THE LAST
    Discussed.   2 Pt.3:3
    Measured differently by God and man. Two ways.   2 Pt.3:8

TRIALS - TRIBULATION (See **SUFFERING; TEMPTATION**)
    Deliverance through. God knows how to deliver.   2 Pt.2:9

TRUTH
    Abuse of.   2 Pt.2:10-22

UNBELIEF
    Fallacies of. Discussed.   2 Pt.3:4; 3:5-7
    In what. In the return of Christ and judgment.   2 Pt.3:1-7; 3:8-10

UNBELIEVER (See **UNSAVED**)
    Meaning. Those who scoff at the supernatural - ignorant of.   2 Pt.3:1-7
    Wrong of. Scoff at supernatural.   2 Pt.3:1-7

UNFRUITFUL - UNFRUITFULNESS
    Discussed.   2 Pt.1:8-11

OUTLINE & SUBJECT INDEX

OUTLINE & SUBJECT INDEX

ILLUSTRATION INDEX

2 PETER

ILLUSTRATION INDEX

ILLUSTRATION INDEX

ILLUSTRATION INDEX

Purpose Statement

Leadership Ministries Worldwide

exists to equip ministers, teachers, and laymen in their
understanding, preaching, and teaching of God's Word
by publishing and distributing worldwide
The Preacher's Outline & Sermon Bible®
and related *Outline* Bible materials,
to reach & disciple men, women, boys, and girls for Jesus Christ.

• Mission Statement •

1. To make the Bible so understandable - its truth so clear and plain - that men
   and women everywhere, whether teacher or student, preacher or hearer,
   can grasp its Message and receive Jesus Christ as Savior; and...
2. To place the Bible in the hands of all who will preach and teach God's Holy
   Word, verse by verse, precept by precept, regardless of the individual's
   ability to purchase it.

The *Outline* Bible materials have been given to LMW for printing and especially
distribution worldwide at/below cost, by those who remain anonymous. One fact,
however, is as true today as it was in the time of Christ:

• The Gospel is free, but the cost of taking it is not •

LMW depends on the generous gifts of Believers with a heart for Him and a love and
burden for the lost. They help pay for the printing, translating, and placing *Outline*
Bible materials in the hands and hearts of those worldwide who will present God's
message with clarity, authority and understanding beyond their own.

LMW was incorporated in the state of Tennessee in July 1992 and received IRS 501(c) 3 nonprofit status in March 1994. LMW is an international, nondenominational mission organization.
All proceeds from USA sales, along with donations from donor partners, go 100% into under-
writing our translation and distribution projects of *Outline* Bible materials to preachers,
church & lay leaders, and Bible students around the world.

9/98   © 1998. Leadership Ministries Worldwide

Box 21310 - Chattanooga, TN 37424 • (423) 855-2181 • FAX (423) 855-8616
• E-Mail - outlinebible@compuserve.com — www.outlinebible.org •

Equipping God's Servants Worldwide

1. **PAYMENT PLANS.** Convenient and affordable ways to get/use your FullSet with easy payments.

2. **NEW TESTAMENT.** In 14 volumes. Deluxe version 3-ring binders. Also: SoftBound Set, 3 volume set, and NIV edition. All on 1 CD-ROM disc.

3. **OLD TESTAMENT.** In process; 1 volume releases about every 6-8 months, in sequence.

4. **THE MINISTERS HANDBOOK.** Acclaimed as a "must-have" for every minister or Christian worker. Outlines more than 400 verses into topics like Power, Victory, Encouragement, Security, Restoration, etc. Discount for quantities.

5. *THE TEACHER'S OUTLINE & STUDY BIBLE.* Verse-by-verse study & teaching; 45 minute lesson or session. Ideal for study, small groups, classes, even home schooling. Each book also offers a STUDENT JOURNAL for study members.

6. **OUTLINE BIBLE CD-ROM.** Includes all current volumes and books; Preacher, Teacher, and Minister Handbook. 1 disc. WORDsearch STEP format. Also 50+ Bible study tools unlockable on same disc. **FREE Downloads - www.outlinebible.org**

7. **THE OUTLINE.** Quarterly newsletter to all users and owners of *POSB.* Complimentary.

8. **LMW AGENT PLAN.** An exciting way any user sells *OUTLINE* materials & earns a second income.

9. **DISTRIBUTION.** Our ultimate mission is to provide *POSB* volumes & materials to preachers, pastors, national church leaders around the world. This is especially for those unable to purchase at U.S. price. USA sales gain goes 100% to provide volumes at affordable prices within the local economy.

10. **TRANSLATIONS.** Korean, Russian, & Spanish are shipping first volumes — a great effort and expense. Hindi, Chinese, French, + 5 others in process.

11. **FUNDING PARTNERS.** To cover the cost of all the translations, plus print, publish, and distribute around the world is a multi million dollar project.

    Church-to-Church Partners send *Outline* Bible books to their missionaries, overseas church leaders, Bible Institues and seminaries...at special prices.

12. **REFERRALS.** Literally thousands (perhaps even you!) first heard of *POSB* from a friend. Now Referral Credit pays $16.00 for each new person who orders from a customer's Referral.

13. **CURRICULUM & COPYRIGHT.** Permission may be given to copy specific portions of *POSB* for special group situations. Write/FAX for details.

9/98

For Information about any of the above, kindly FAX, E-Mail, Call, or Write

Please PRAY 1 Minute/Day for LMW!

PO Box 21310, Chattanooga, TN 37424 • (423) 855-2181 • FAX (423) 855-8616
• E-Mail - outlinebible@compuserve.com — www.outlinebible.org •

Sharing

With the World!